CW00733112

# PRACTICAL

# Garden Railways

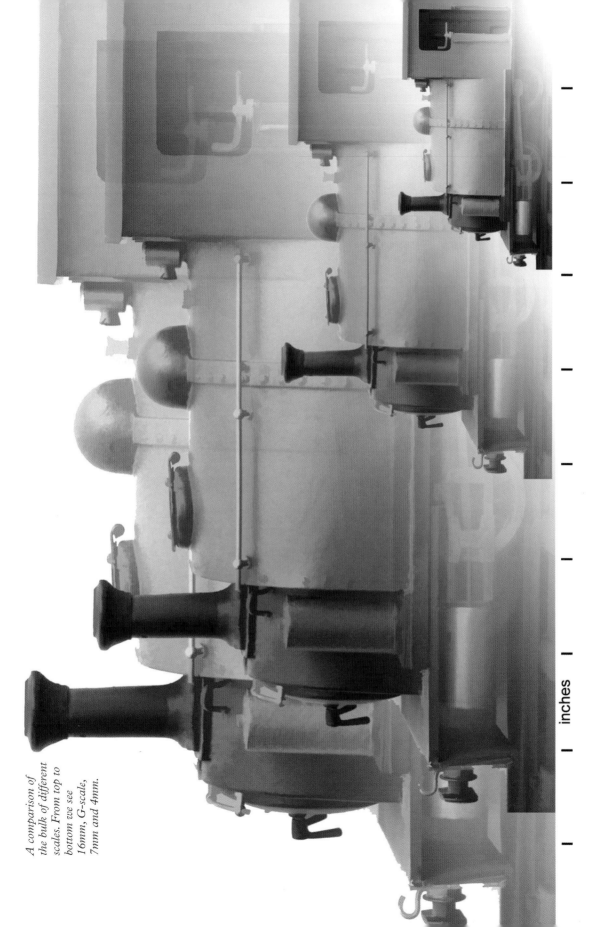

*A comparison of the bulk of different scales. From top to bottom we see 16mm, G-scale, 7mm and 4mm.*

inches

# PRACTICAL

# Garden Railways

## Peter Jones

The Crowood Press

First published in 2006 by
The Crowood Press Ltd
Ramsbury, Marlborough
Wiltshire SN8 2HR

**www.crowood.com**

© Peter Jones 2006

All rights reserved. No part of this publication may be reproduced or
transmitted in any form or by any means, electronic or mechanical, including
photocopy, recording, or any information storage and retrieval system, without
permission in writing from the publishers.

**British Library Cataloguing-in-Publication Data**
A catalogue record for this book is available from the British Library.

ISBN    1 86126 833 5
EAN     978 1 86126 833 4

Cover illustration by Michael O'Hara.

Typeset by Servis Filmsetting Ltd, Manchester

Printed and bound in Singapore by Craft Print International

# Contents

# Foreword

The pastime of garden railways is one of the most engaging and rewarding activities one can pursue, combining the immensely popular hobbies of gardening and model railways in all their various aspects. It knows no national boundaries and is enjoyed by people around the globe. It is practised by men, women and children of all ages, and is the perfect family activity. This is an exceptionally broad and deep endeavour, one in which you will never hit bottom, and it offers something for everyone.

There is nothing new about garden railways. They have been around in one form or another for well over a century. The first commercial model trains were on the largish side, better suited for outdoor spaces. That applied doubly for those that actually ran on steam, where the danger of setting the carpet alight was both real and present. The earliest trains also tended to be expensive, so many of the first outdoor model railways were owned by the wealthy and operated by the gardener.

As model trains became cheaper and more accessible, they began to appeal more to the masses, and a great hobby came into being. Garden railways declined in popularity at the end of the Second World War, but experienced the beginnings of a steady renaissance in the late 1960s. Today, the hobby is alive and vibrant. We are living in a golden age of garden railways, supported by a vast number of commercial products, many clubs and associations, and several fine periodicals, published in different countries.

Peter Jones, the author of the book you are now holding, has been a garden railwayman for the better part of half a century, and he and I have been friends and associates for close on twenty-five years. Peter is the ideal person to have written this book. His vast experience in, and undying devotion to, garden railways puts him well ahead of almost everyone else out there. His own garden line, the well-known and widely published Compton Down railway, has been around in one form or another for some forty years. Peter's unorthodox and creative approach to the hobby, as well as his willingness – almost to extremes – to help 'spread the word', as it were, by expounding on his techniques and methods in print and in person, has been a boon to countless other adherents of all ages and levels of experience. So there you are. Read this book, enjoy it, learn from it, and become involved. You'll be pleased that you did and I'm sure you'll never look back.

Marc Horovitz
Founding Editor, *Garden Railways Magazine*
March 2005

# Acknowledgements

All photographs are by the author unless otherwise credited. Many people and organizations were extremely supportive of the writing of this book, and I thank them all. But I would like to single out Dave Rowlands: a very long-standing friend who has been such a force for good to garden railways, and who has also had to suffer many years of being a sounding-board for the fruits of my fevered brain. I should like to thank Eric Lloyd, Terry Collins, Alan Craney, Brian Spring, Dave Lomas, Don Jones, Ron Brown, Marty Cozad, Alan Millichamp and Phil Beckey for their garden railways, illustrations of which appear in this book. Phil, in particular, provided some excellent photographs of the sort of railway I would like to build if I were not devoted to my narrow gauge. I am grateful too for the kind assistance of Marc Horovitz, Bill Basey, Tag Gorton and Gareth Jones. Further thanks are due to Andrew Pullen of Aster UK for generous permission to use official drawings and photographs. The various scale societies were most helpful and, in this regard, I thank Geoff Calver, Paul Cooper, Ian Turner and John Evans. Special thanks must go to Manfred Meliset for generously allowing me to use photographs from *Die Gartenbahn* magazine. Judy Jones should be warmly thanked for her lovely traditional draughtsmanship – and also for putting up with being Mrs Jones all these years. Denys Bassett-Jones produced the diagrams in the book, and I offer my grateful thanks. Any omissions from this list are my fault entirely and I apologize for them. The way that everyone rallied round to help me was a testament to the camaraderie of this hobby.

It may be useful to acknowledge some of the influences from the past that shaped my thinking. The book *Railway Adventure* by L.T.C. Rolt inspired in me a lifetime of enthusiasm; and 'Curly' Lawrence, who, under his pen name of 'LBSC', wrote in such a friendly and encouraging way about model engineering that he made people, myself included, believe that they could accomplish much. I hope he would have approved of the unstuffy tone of this book. Whilst I was brought up on a diet of the old model-railway writers like Beal, Wickham and Carter, it was John Ahern who really shaped the way I interpreted railways in model form. His Madder Valley railway, part of which holds a special place of honour at Pendon Museum in Oxfordshire, was the indoor equivalent of what I always wanted my garden railway to be.

# CHAPTER 1

# Introduction

This is not just a book for beginners: it is also for wishful thinkers who would like to be beginners.

Welcome to the world of garden railways. In these pages we are going to immerse ourselves in the spirit of the subject and then, together, we will look at the details. You will come to realize that there is no magic involved: just a series of achievable adventures to be enjoyed. And the first thing to do is realize that this isn't just one hobby: it can be a hundred different hobbies – each one unique to the individual. Neither is it a subject that can easily be defined in black and white terms. I can suggest things that work well and those that don't. But there will be others who see things differently yet enjoy the hobby as much as I do. Thus we speak of tendencies and approaches. This is a hobby relatively free of pedants. Instead it consists mostly of people who enjoy themselves.

Many of the illustrations were taken from my railway, or those of a few friends. But that's all they are: illustrations. I like well-weathered narrow gauge trains and muted colours. Your taste may be for pristine models, straight from the box. But no matter what the scale or the ambience may be, the principles of garden railways remain the same. You will translate them into your railway.

Running a model railway through a garden is an honourable tradition almost as old as passenger-carrying railways themselves. As early as 1847, Tennyson wrote in his poem, *The Princess*: 'Round the lake, a little clockwork steamer paddling, plied and shook the lilies; perch'd about the knolls a dozen angry models jetted steam; a petty railway ran . . .' and you can be sure that this situation hadn't come about there and then. It had to have taken time to develop to that stage.

The earliest practical model loco design I know of was built in 1833. It had a boiler 10in (25cm) long and the ¾in (2cm) diameter piston drove the axle through spur gearing. In the light of today's experience, the designer missed a trick in making both gears the same size. A decent speed reduction on those wheels would have been useful. Steam was generated by a red-hot piece of iron being pushed into a flue tube. In quiet moments I have often wondered about building a replica to see how it performed. But the lure of being outside with the garden railway has proved too strong thus far.

(Photo: Geoff Culver)

*A hobby for all seasons.
(Photo: Phil Beckey)*

*A garden railway can have
dramatic moments too. This
night-time shot was taken of
the author's coking plant in
16mm scale.*

Down the decades, the attraction of running a real
railway through a real landscape has evolved with
technology, although the appeal has remained
essentially the same.

That aforementioned petty railway was probably
built to order and would have represented some
fine engineering. By today's standards it might be
considered somewhat crude, but all the basic elements were there. We are not sure how petty it was,
but it could well have been something that had a
gauge of several inches. From such simple beginnings, the live steam engine – and hence the garden

railway – evolved through two separate routes.

First, there were models that were craftsman-
made and very expensive. It is no coincidence that
the roll-call of early garden railway pioneers contained many titled persons. The engines and rolling
stock would have been commissioned from someone versed in fine engineering. This tradition con-
tinued well into the twentieth century. It was partly
democratized by the emerging model manufacturers who were equipped for rudimentary production
lines, and thus able to bring down costs in real
terms.

*The mass-produced simple toy at its most basic. Because of the wheel configuration, these are known as 'stork legs'.*

*Primitive origins.*

*Manufacturers were quite ingenious at producing a working steam loco with the minimum possible number of parts . . .*

*. . . but these basics could be refined and extended. We are starting to get a slightly more realistic appearance now.*

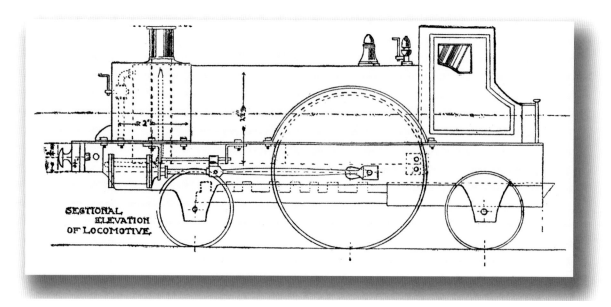

*Here is a 1908 design for a simple steam locomotive that could be built at home with hand tools. You were enjoined to purchase the machine wheels and cylinders from Messrs Stuart Turner.*

The other resource was the toy manufacturer. Cheap tinplate trains could be run in the garden. Indeed, with their tendency towards self-destruction by fire, they were a lot safer there! The story of the early toy train makers is a fascinating one and it can form a lifetime's hobby in its own right. British, and particularly German, toymakers formed much of the foundation of practical garden railways as we know them today. In particular, at the end of the nineteenth century, the 'Model Dockyards' were a source of practical and functional equipment.

Meanwhile, the hobby of model engineering was gaining ground. Simple castings and drawings became available. Typically a 2½in gauge engine would be fired by a vaporizing paraffin burner. It would haul an adult on an elevated track or pull a rake of model coaches. The *Model Engineer* magazine was founded, with its appeal directly aimed at competent metalworkers and craftsmen. Into this scene came a man who transformed live steam locomotive building and set out the whole future of the hobby. 'Curly' Lawrence, under his pen name of LBSC, developed the high-pressure coal-fired model locomotive as a practical proposition for building at home. He did so in the teeth of some reactionary opposition, and even today there

remain underlying currents of discord. But, as previously mentioned, Lawrence wrote in such a friendly way as to convince you that you *could* build a locomotive.

Whilst this was happening to model engineering, the broader aspects of garden railways were gaining ground. Toymakers offered options of higher quality and were becoming good model railway suppliers in their own right. For example, we have a lot to thank Bassett-Lowke for. They made garden railways accessible to a wider following. The durability of some of their products could be amazing. I have a 16mm tank loco that I built in 1953, and the B-L electric motor that drives it dates back to the 1930s. It is still running well. Around 1949 Ray Tustin wrote *Garden Railways*. It was regarded as a definitive work for its time and it still makes for an interesting read today if you can get hold of a copy.

Perhaps I could be forgiven a personal note here. As a very small boy I had a 0-gauge tinplate railway, mostly by Hornby. The locos were clockwork driven and it all had good play value. My first garden railway locomotive consisted of a crude 16mm scale body, built over one of my Hornby engines. It did not survive but I did build a replica many years later. My first Compton Down Railway was built by pushing tinplate track into the ground, between

# BASSETT-LOWKE LTD

# Mogul 2-6-0 Locomotive and Tender
## (STEAM)

*Since this model was first produced, it has set a standard of excellent appearance and good performance. It follows closely Sir William Stanier's prototype designs and because of the refinements of control it is a delightful machine to operate.*

*The 2-6-0, or Mogul type locomotive may be described as the "Jack of all trades" in allocating locomotives to their daily tasks. It is used on fast and slow goods, is ideal for excursions and relief trains, and even on fast passenger trains in the case of emergency. The present model, as shown, is based on the ex-L.M.S. design by Sir William Stanier, with tapered boiler. All four groups of the British Railways possessed a number of these useful engines before nationalisation and a new design is included in the B.R. standard types now in the course of construction.*

No. 6661/0                                     Price **£25. 10. 0.**

## Specification

**Frames, Footplate and Superstructure.** Pressed steel plate.

**Wheels.** Modern locomotive design with crescent shaped balance weights. Made in fine cast-iron, finished dull nickel.

**Boiler.** Cylindrical brass with copper steam pipes, tested to 45 lb. per sq. inch. Fired by vaporizing spirit lamp.

**Cylinders and Motion.** Piston valve cylinders of hard brass and brass piston rods. Stainless steel piston valves. Greenly-Walschaert valve gear, reversing from cab, exhaust into chimney.

**Fittings.** Combined safety valve and filler under dome. Whistle in cab. Regulator handle protruding through cab roof.

**Lubrication.** Cylinder lubricated by automatic displacement lubricator.

**Tender.** Of standard pattern with six wheels, standard flanges and finished in dull nickel. Cast dummy springs to axle boxes.

**Finish.** Supplied hand finished in B.R. livery.

**Length.** 18 in.     **Weight.** 3 lb. 8 oz.

*Page Nineteen*

---

*A page from a later Bassett-Lowke catalogue. Appearances have come a long way. It is interesting to note the rise of interest in modern reproductions of Bassett-Lowke technology.*

| | | | | |
|---|---|---|---|---|
| **A ROUGH GUIDE TO SCALES AND GAUGES** | | | | |
| **Scale** | **Proportion** | **Ratio** | **Gauge** | **Notes** |
| H09 | 1.87 | 3.5mm:1ft | narrow | Widespread in Europe |
| H0 | 1.87 | 3.5mm:1ft | standard | Widespread in Europe and USA |
| 009 | 1.76 | 4mm:1ft | narrow | British practice |
| 00 | 1.76 | 4mm :1ft | standard | |
| 0.16.5 | 1.43 | 7mm:1ft | narrow | |
| 0 | 1.43 | 7mm:1ft | standard | Often ¼in:1ft in USA |
| 1 | 1.32 | 10mm:1ft | standard | Common equivalent in USA is 1.29 scale |
| G | 1.22.5 | varies | narrow | Also a muddle of scales including 1.20.3. 1.24. 1.25 |
| 16mm | 1.19 | 16mm:1ft | narrow | Also seems to include 14mm:1ft. Often known as SM32 or SM45, depending on which gauge is used (usually SM32) |
| 2½in or gauge 3 | varies | varies | standard (2½in) | Treat it as an approximate standard gauge equivalent of 16mm and G scale. One term you may encounter is G64 |

This table has been horribly simplified but should be enough to present an approximate picture. Although some manufacturers continue to compound the muddle, do not despair. It does become clear as you immerse yourself in the hobby.

*An illustration of a late nineteenth-century design from Stevens Model Dockyard . . .*

plants, in a rockery, until just the railtops showed. I had only a child's skill and frugal pocket money so everything had to be home-made. I am still reaping the rewards of that practical apprenticeship a lifetime later. It also gave me a first awareness of the changing atmosphere that a garden railway can offer in such abundance.

Early on a summer morning, there is a sense of expectancy when steam is being raised on a railway

*. . . and here it is, being restored, in the flesh. It seems massive and crude compared to 16mm scale track, but you have to concede its imperial bearing.*

*Bringing our brief historical overview to an end is this picture of an 0-gauge live steam locomotive, built by Archangel Models in the late 1960s. Such things heralded well-engineered, high-pressure steam locomotives that had a scale appearance but which were affordable.*

*Our predecessors gave us the foundations on which we can build our garden railways today. Phil Beckey's two-rail 0-gauge line blends in with its surroundings nicely. (Photo: Phil Beckey)*

engine. At such times the difference between the model and the full-size prototype can seem very small indeed. We all seem to have our own favourite 'atmospheres'. Mine revolves around those dull quiet afternoons of late autumn when there is not a breath of wind and the birds do not sing. Somewhere on the air is the smell of burning leaves, and the sound of a tiny train puffing and rumbling through the afternoon landscape may be clearly heard. But midsummer dawns, dark nights under lights and baking hot afternoons all have their appeal; an appeal that we can share in. This is our world; a world where things are done differently.

## EXPLODING MYTHS

Right at the outset, let's get rid of a few myths. A neat garden is not essential: neither is a level site. In many respects, a garden with some sort of gradient or some humps and hollows can be a positive advantage: something to be exploited. There are ways round most supposed difficulties. My friend Dave Lomas has built a lovely railway in Hawaii. It is in a rampant tropical rainforest on a 45-degree slope of volcanic ash. So you have no excuse! In the main, there are few reasons why a garden railway cannot be built. We don't need a fat wallet or a degree in engineering. Neither a fully

*The addition of live steam brings more work but extra atmosphere.*

*Live steam adds to the early morning mist. The sun is just starting to break through in this slightly dreamy picture.*

Ordinary tools found around the house will cope with most of our needs. The secret to using them is to keep them in good condition. So don't begrudge buying a decent saw, for example. A spirit level and a tape measure are needed. In the case of the spirit level, if you want someone to treat you to a birthday present, drop hints for one fitted with a laser. But it isn't essential. There are some of us who have managed with bits of garden hose and plastic tube for many a year. Let us assume that you have the usual modest collection of DIY tools, and that you also know how to use them, without necessarily being a skilled cabinetmaker. So there is no need in this book for a diagram showing how a saw is held.

*Garden railways don't have to be only about attractive plants and landscapes. Natural light can work well on an industrial setting too.*

*Keeping things simple: a ground level part of Alan Millichamp's railway crosses the path.*

equipped workshop nor endless patience is required. If you have any of the above then so much the better but people seem to get by without. If you can draw a straight line with a ruler and you can measure a right angle, you are in business.

'There is only one difficult job in building a garden railway: making a start . . . after that the rest is easy.' (Me: *circa* 1958)

*The large scale of 2½in gauge needs a lot of space to sweep around. But it can give a lovely nostalgic feel when done just right. (Photo: courtesy 2½in Association)*

## SOME OF THE CHOICES

The garden railway is a peculiar beast that comes in all sorts of sub-species. For guidance, let's run through a few crude headings. Right down at (literally) grass roots level, we join some sections of track together, and put them on the grass or the patio. A train is set going and it is all very pleasant. The author is as guilty of enjoying this as anyone else. The next step is to run the track through the rockery and to try to blend the track into the landscape. This is aesthetically pleasing but still rather temporary. We soon realize that smooth running and durability may be lacking. So thoughts turn to more reliable foundations that will still blend into the natural landscape. For ease of operation, we can raise the track a little, to run on low walls made of natural stone. Plants may then be arranged to harmonize with this. The act of surveying and building a model railway through the natural countryside is not modelling as such: it is the real thing writ small.

It is all too easy to become carried away with this technique. Waist-high walls of natural stone and brick sweep around the garden, with raised flower-beds and plantings. Instead of blending the layout into the garden, it becomes the starting point for creating something entirely in its own right. The garden becomes a location in which to build a model railway. Human nature is such that, if you ask anyone the best way to build a garden railway, they will usually tell you that theirs is. Rest assured, I shall avoid that trap and simply tell you what has worked for me. You can then make up your own mind.

The other common form of layout building is based around some sort of elevated decking supported on uprights. If it is not too high, natural greenery can be trained to disguise this, but there comes a point where it becomes a separate feature in the garden, standing tall and proud.

*One of the choices we have is to enjoy the craft of model making to its utmost. This is modelling for its own sake.*

*There is a warm glow to this late summer evening. Up in the trees the rooks have stopped squabbling but a blackbird is still singing lustily. On this raised trackbed, the trains still run on at our command. (Photo: Geoff Culver)*

*A simple raised timber trackbed is surrounded by natural plant life. This 0-gauge layout is a piece of magic for small eyes. (Photo: John Evans)*

Perhaps this is a good time to introduce another factor for you to think about. Although not inevitable, there is a divide between modelling little narrow gauge railways and mainline standard gauge. The latter is often a world of large express engines hauling long trains smoothly over large sweeping curves. Narrow gauge railways, particularly popular in the garden, are more about little tank engines swaying through a bucolic world where time isn't terribly important. There is a tendency for this difference to be reflected in the way that the railway is built: a sort of philosophical divide. It is noticeable that narrow gauge modellers, whatever scales they work in, tend to congregate together in larger herds to graze on the sunny uplands of their own particular interests.

## A FEELING FOR SIZE AND SPACE

What the garden does offer us is *space* . . . lots of it. So we can work in a large scale. Later on you will find descriptions of the various scales and gauges, but the greater part of this work will centre round what have been called the 'garden gauges'. A simple tank engine might be 8–12in (20–30cm) long and be a comfortable chunky lift between two hands. For years, in my wallet, I carried a little cardboard cut-out of a man in the scale I worked in whose job it was to help me check the size of toy figures and vehicles that I encountered in cut-price shops and junk stalls. He was just under 4in (10cm) high. So for practical purposes let us assume that sort of degree of chunkiness in our thinking and planning.

There is absolutely no reason why smaller scales cannot be used in the garden. Indeed, there are some good reasons why you might care to examine this option. If you want to build an N gauge layout in a large window box that sits on a balcony, then by all means do so and enjoy it. Equally, you could take advantage of a large garden to run tiny models of huge US freight trains in a space that does them justice. There is even a school of thought that speaks of building small outdoor layouts in metal trays. A small western desert railway running through cactus plants is a typical option.

*The trains themselves can be a smaller part of the picture: sometimes barely visible in the landscape. It is a way of capturing and recapturing that feeling of 'each a glimpse and gone forever'.*

The upper limit of the scale of model railways in the garden is harder to define. It begins to merge into the world of model engineering where the emphasis changes to that of hauling full-size passengers behind the working, coal-fired, steam locomotive that is the focus of the hobby. The agenda for the model engineer is subtly different and is catered for by its own press. However, the boundary between the two hobbies is not rigid. Larger, model-engineering scales have been used for scenic railway modelling, so it is worth being receptive to all sorts of influences and ideas.

We shall try to avoid talking about better or worse sorts of garden railway. It is a broad church, based on the fact that we get pleasure and enjoyment from what we do. If your simple circuit of plastic track is surrounded by garden gnomes, whose company you enjoy, then your railway is as worthwhile as that of the pernickety fine-scale modeller who insists on total accuracy. But there is also no place for inverted snobbery. His perfection will bring him equal pleasure. We shall concentrate on what works well and what does not, casting an eye over the pleasures and the pitfalls of it all. But throughout, we will be under that ever-changing sky, watching the year turn. Ours is a world of unfolding days; time to dream, and time to imagine a world where dew-covered spider's webs are as important as rivet detail on the engines: time to begin.

## AMERICANA

*Backwoods Americana personified in this logging locomotive.*

Most of what you will read here is based around British practice. Much of this translates nicely into European practice, particularly in respect of narrow gauge. But railways from the USA (and its exports) have quite a different feel about them and deserve a section to themselves. I have a seen a full-size tiny branch line (short line) of unfenced, beat-up track, which is run as a railway from someone's house. When some freight cars need to carry a load or two along it, the owner of the company phones round to find an engine for the job. His brother drives the train down the line and, after unloading, he is paid in dollar bills by the recipient. It is not unusual to see a freight train left outside a roadside café, engine running, whilst the crew have their lunch. Yes, there are some seriously run mainline trains in the USA but much of the backwater railroading lends itself nicely to being modelled in the garden.

Trackwork is often to a lower standard than British eyes would be used to. It is spiked directly into sometimes rather weary sleepers (ties), so there is a characteristic of spacing them closer together. The unevenness would be a strain on the rigidity of a conventional plate-frame locomotive. This is why locos in the USA have a distinctive, spindly look in their lower portions, deriving from the bar frames (and why passenger and freight cars run on bogies instead of fixed wheelsets). Because of the system of train control by orders, signals are much rarer. Indeed, most small-town engine design is pure function. The cowcatcher (pilot) is there because the lack of trackside fencing allows animals to be on the line. It is noteworthy that very few US locomotives are named. To me, this symbolizes the different ethoses of the two countries.

## AMERICANA *continued*

*In this picture you can almost feel the intense heat. The engineer is grateful for his air-conditioned cab. 1:29th scale by Marty Cozad. (Photo: Marc Horovitz)*

Large tracts of the USA have lumber as the main resource for building. So instead of brick viaducts we may well encounter timber trestle bridges. The old cowboy Wild West town wasn't built like that to look good in the movies; it was what was easiest and cheapest to build. All of these features affect the way a US garden railway will look.

G scale dominates the hobby, and the advent of budget-priced equipment from the likes of Bachmann has encouraged it even further. There is still a tendency, in some quarters, towards rabbit-warren layouts with very sharp curves. But, as we discussed early on, if it gives pleasure to its owners, that is all that matters. Another, somewhat basic alternative is to erect sometimes huge test tracks that are purely functional. Live steam engines, often in 1/29th, or the nearby 10mm scale, standard gauge (G1) haul big trains around, and this is the beginning and end of the hobby for its adherents.

The USA, however, can give us inspiration for wonderfully atmospheric garden railways. Comfortably aged trains that ooze character can serve all those weathered wood buildings. There is a whole sub-hobby of forestry railways (timber roads) with Shays and Heislers built to work on poor tracks. The early western railroads need no introduction. Ready to run equipment is available for this and we can re-create the whole picture. The Clancy Gang can ride again!

A modern form of this could be the present day short line where small diesel locos (gas switchers) run short freights and a few passenger cars from one part of our dream world to another, or just go happily round in circles, capturing our imagination. But whatever the format, the mechanics of building it are particularly easy. With so much literature and trade support, most of the problems have long since been ironed out and written up. The superb *Garden Railways* magazine seems to tell us everything we may need to know – including links to extensive Internet resources. For a more specialist interest, *Steam in the Garden* magazine does exactly what it says on the tin.

*A budget price 1:29th scale two-rail diesel shunting loco (gas switcher). Don Jones has done a lovely weathering job on this plastic model, using 'scale colour'.*

As you turn these pages you will start to get a feel of that broad base to the subject. There is equal pleasure for the craftsman and for someone with ten thumbs. What can't be built can be bought, and what can't be afforded can usually be got round somehow or another. There is scope for the technocrat and the artist: the lazy and the workaholic. But, above all, there is scope for the dreamer in all of us.

*This Bulleid Pacific has a glassfibre shell and can be bought as a machined kit. Some tweaking may be needed but hand tools should cover most things. It will be expensive but, of course, represents virtually all of your outlay.*

O.16.5 track

standard gauge
2-rail...

irregular surface

facing wall

soil pockets
for heathers >>

# CHAPTER 2

# Planning

That blank piece of paper in front of you can be rather daunting, so get straight on with filling in some priorities and requirements. A good starting point is the situation, as it is, before building actually starts. So describe the garden to yourself. Is it sloping or flat? Is it large or small? How secure is it? How exposed to the elements is it? Do other members of the family jealously guard its integrity? Is it boggy? Is it an untamed wilderness? It is a great help if you can get a plan of the garden fixed in your mind

at an early stage. So get the tape measure out and make a rough scale drawing on paper. In time, the size and shape will become carved into your heart. Set about listing any particular problems peculiar to your garden. Here are a few actual examples: wandering moose and caribou (not a common problem in Wimbledon), permafrost heave, inner-city gang warfare, black bears, your children on bikes, skunks, public footpaths through the site, flooding, alligators, earthquakes, and finally: council officials. All of these problems are solvable.

Next, time to roughly outline what sort of railway you want. Typically you might aim for a modest narrow gauge railway that blends in with the existing garden. There wants to be minimal disturbance to the garden but the foundations should be well thought out, so that the whole thing isn't going to become an overgrown and unusable eyesore in twelve months' time. You may share my view that the railway should be available for use throughout the year, in all weathers, day or night, and be comfortable to operate. There is the convenience factor

to consider. It makes more sense, given a choice, to have the centre of operations close to the back door of your house, rather than at the far end of the garden. If there is a prevailing wind direction, try to organize things so that there is some sort of shelter against it.

*A modest narrow gauge railway that blends in with the garden.*

*Thoughts about prevailing winds might cross your mind when you plan. (Photo: Brian Spring)*

You might think about where the sunniest part of the garden is, or perhaps consider something as mundane as the location of a clothesline. Certainly, it is always a good tactic to take the family with you in your ambitions. Don't present them with grand plans that involve major excavations and chaos. One way of avoiding strained family relationships is to plant a couple of yards of track, sympathetically, in the rockery. Given watering and care, it is amazing how this plant – *Floribunda ferroequinologica* – can mysteriously grow over the years. Try to avoid the need for railway tracks to cross existing footpaths. If this cannot be avoided, there are straightforward ways to tackle it. When the plan is for an end-to-end layout, running beside a couple of boundary walls, this is rarely a problem. But a good percentage of successful layouts incorporate a complete circuit, so that the trains can run without constant attention; particularly important if you want

to enjoy live steam operation. You can put a small circle of track in one corner of your garden, but you will then miss one of the main attractions of the outdoor railway: great long sweeping curves that run boldly through your three-dimensional canvas. If you have space to play with, it seems a shame not to use it.

## SECURITY

Whilst you are doodling our thoughts on to the page, you should consider security. A back garden, out of sight of the public, is the best setting. If it can be protected by at least one locked door, so much the better. If the garden is visible to the outside world then try to arrange for the lines of sight to be obscured. None of this is essential but it gives added peace of mind against vandalism. Should the site be vulnerable then plan accordingly. In the case of an exposed urban site, it may make sense just to concrete down some plain track and remove anything else when it is not in use. Thorny bushes will deter people who would like to climb over fences but make sure that the thorns don't keep stabbing you at the same time. On the subject of security: a tip. Never be tempted to publicize your railway in a local newspaper or TV station. You will probably be described as an eccentric (which in the case of some of us may be true) but your address will be given out to any hooligan looking for a fresh challenge. Your garden railway will soon become known amongst your fellow enthusiasts anyway.

## PETS

Do you have pets? If so, think about them and their endearing characteristics. The usual danger is the happy, enthusiastic dog that plays in the garden with unconfined rapture. Bridges across paths mean nothing to him whatsoever. It is his garden as much as yours, so plan accordingly. Cats will delicately use your trackbed as a convenient path. However, their sanitary arrangements may not be to your liking. Your own cat may well be trainable but visiting felines might need special attention. In the past I have got into trouble for humorously

*The sort of railway that starts simple and mysteriously grows. This area started out as a single track on a wooden shelf.*

suggesting ingenious ways of dealing with cats. The kind answer seems to be to buy one of those hypersonic cat-scarers. I once tried to combine a garden railway with owning a goat – a bad idea – the beast had no sense of discipline whatsoever.

If you have large animals as neighbours, make sure that the fences are proof against them. One of my more interesting experiences was having a herd of cattle get on to my garden railway, only to be rounded up by several people on horseback – not recommended.

One subtler planning problem concerns wild birds. Do take note if you have any power or telephone lines crossing your garden overhead. They may well provide perches for large numbers of birds in a string. It is not a good idea to have fine-scale structures, carefully painted, underneath. Neither is it a good idea for you to have an operating area for yourself there. Likewise, don't hang a bird feeder directly about your steam-up area. The best advice I ever heard on this topic was that it is not a good idea to use sudden loud noises to scare the birds away: this merely makes the white blobs bigger!

If you have an interest in attracting wildlife to your garden, then you will already know what works and what does not. For example you will realize that putting out too much food for birds at ground level can also attract rats and mice. Even if you like to have a tidy garden, there can still be a neatly bounded area that is populated with wild grasses and nettles. When you have a railway, you get a much closer vision of your garden. The ecology of it becomes more significant. On a damp, late evening, the sudden appearance of a toad on your trackbed certainly lifts the spirit.

## DIVERSE THOUGHTS ON SHEDS

It makes sense to have that operating area in a convenient place. It is easier to fiddle with trains, especially live steam engines, if you can do so at a comfortable height. You may be able to exploit the natural slope of a garden, using a retaining wall to arrange this. If possible, try to organize things so that the place where you store railway stock is fairly convenient to where you put it on the track.

My father always reckoned that the secret of a happy marriage was to get a shed. He was right. It is especially true if you want a convenient garden railway. At the very least it is somewhere to store stock that, in the case of garden gauges, can be quite bulky (fit a decent padlock please). It is also, of course, a workshop – although it has to be said that there are some weaker brethren amongst us whose workshop equipment consists of little more than an old armchair and a fridge! You can run tracks into the workshop through little hatches. While this cuts out stock handling, tracks down at ankle level are nicely situated for accidentally kicking your stock, spilling paint and sawdust, or dropping bricks on it.

*Track that simply runs through a hedge on a timber support is unobtrusive and gives the natural wildlife space to become a principal attraction.*

*A convenient height has many obvious operating advantages. (Photo: Geoff Culver)*

Sheds come in all shapes and sizes. Don't expect too much from the cheap, nailed-together thing that has inadequate space for cat-swinging. Apart from anything else, no matter how good your padlock, your valuable steam locomotives can be just one quick flick of a crowbar away from being history. But simple wooden sheds have a lot going for them. Condensation is less of a problem and it is easy to fit extra ventilation to allow a cool flow of air on very hot days. One useful tip concerns any roof that is covered with roofing felt. Paint it over with white or cream masonry paint. It makes it much cooler on hot days and provides extra life to the felt.

The better option is to be able to arrange things so that the track comes in at waist level. Then, as well as storage, it can be turned into part of the

---

If you want to improve lines of sight out of a simple wooden shed (for example, to be able to view a particular section of track for operational purposes), there is a quick and cheap way of doing this. Buy a small, wooden picture frame. You can probably pick up a small but ghastly picture at a jumble sale for pennies. Cut out a suitable opening in the shed wall and then smear the back of the picture frame with clear silicon sealant before screwing it to the shed to frame the opening. Push the glass into place, from the inside, bedding it in sealant. If it is just a small opening, the glass will be tough enough and there is no security risk.

---

railway itself: an excellent location for the main station. As the tracks come in through an opening cut in the wall, the usual ploy is to form some simple channels outside so that a board can slide down over the hole.

Any form of wooden structure should be kept away from bare earth. At the very least, the base of the shed should sit on some roofing felt or similar, but it is better to have it raised a couple of inches above ground level. Tipping a layer of chippings down will help. But the best foundation is a concrete base. This is particularly important when you start putting heavy machinery in the shed. If you live in a very exposed, gale-prone area, a useful refinement is to set four heavy bolts into the concrete, sticking up. These will protrude through the floor and allow it to be safely bolted down with well-greased nuts and big washers. As well as preventing the risk of the shed shifting, it also contributes to a more secure feeling of rigidity if it is at all flimsy.

A concrete garage is not ideal but is better than nothing. An existing conservatory could be adapted or a lean-to built. With a bit of imagination, these structures can be a positive addition to the garden.

A proper garden railway should be an all-year, all-weather thing. The only weak link is the owner. So in our planning, we will try to make life as civilized as we can. It is easy to build in inaccessibility so we must try to arrange things so that we can

*Sheds don't have to be purely functional. The author built this example to give the garden a bit of a lift.*

reach most of the railway from comfortable paths that are dry underfoot. If possible, these paths should also lead to a sitting area where we can relax and let the world drift quietly by in the company of our trains and good friends.

This all sounds like many factors to juggle. But don't worry; it isn't as bad as it sounds. That blank piece of paper will probably be covered with all sorts of sketches by now. The thoughts are starting to firm up. It helps if you can contact other enthusiasts who have some experience. It is especially useful to be able to *see* the way space is used. Fortunately, this is a very friendly, helpful sort of hobby. Whichever scale you are interested in, contact the association or society connected with it. Browse through a few magazines and make contacts. The Internet can be particularly valuable for this as well. Enjoy the process of building up the knowledge base and let the feel of the hobby seep into your bones.

## PLANNING THE RAILWAY ITSELF

You can now extend your thoughts to the basic shape of the layout. Spend short but frequent periods of time in the garden, peering at it through half-closed eyes. Some people can plan a line entirely on small pieces of paper. I am not one of those. I have always found it helps to prop up various bits of wood in the garden to outline where a station area might be. Run the garden hose out to roughly mark out boundaries. This sort of thing helps to avoid horribly sharp curves or places you just can't reach. Actually, this sort of visualizing is an enjoyable task.

We can dream our dreams. The whole concept of the railway is just starting to come alive.

Anyone coming new to railways has to get used to the idea of just how flat and level track has to be. Gradients that are almost imperceptible to the untrained eye can make running live steam engines a miserable and frustrating process. Given a choice, aim to get everything *very* flat. Subsidence and building errors may spoil this but give it your best shot right from the start. Remember also that sharp curves act as a real drag on a train, so a tight bend at the top of a gradient means that the front half of the train may be squealing round a curve whilst the rest of it will be dragging away nicely. These are the sorts of rules you can break when you become more experienced but, for now, keep thinking seriously flat and level; particularly for steam or battery-powered operation. Another piece of planning advice is that it is not compulsory to fill the garden with the biggest and most complicated railway possible. Running a simple railway is a pleasurable experience; tearing your hair out trying to keep a complicated layout working is not. By all means think about possible extensions later on, but keep it simple for the moment.

It is a mistake to endlessly plan every final detail and then carve it in stone. This assumes that you have all your good ideas at once, that none of them are ever wrong and that you will never get a good idea again. You are bound to find that, as the three-dimensional reality starts to take shape, you will see something different; something that could be a bit better. So be prepared to be flexible. And, for heaven's sake, don't get so bogged down that you never get round to starting. Clear a little space and get a bit of track down. Acquire a wagon or suchlike

*Planning isn't always complicated. Large, flat rectangular areas can be a canvas on which to organize a suitable station layout.*

and see what it looks like set in the garden. It will inspire you and it will also ensure that something is actually happening. In short: don't just sit there, *do* something!

As our little sketches continue, there are one or two technical points to consider. If the railway is to be two-rail electric, we shall need to think about getting the low-voltage supply to the tracks and where to run some conduit to protect the wires. You might also think about running a similar low-voltage 'ring main' against some future need for model lighting. There may be a need to run mains electricity out into the garden or a new workshop. This is the time to think about how it is going to be done.

By now, you might be feeling even more daunted by the list of all these things you need to think about. Don't be. Making drawings and notes on bits of paper is a cheap occupation and, on the whole, quite a pleasant one. Having got things clear in your own mind, you can now settle down to the pleasure of designing the layout, but let us agree a few first principles. There are several distinct types of layout.

**End to End**. As its name suggests, this is a length of track that starts and ends in separate locations, probably having station facilities at both ends. This has the advantage of being like the prototype inasmuch as the railway goes from one place to another.

## ELECTRICAL SAFETY

Let us be quite clear about this: there must be no compromises with running mains electricity out of doors. If you can't do it according to proper practice, then get help from someone who can. Correct earthing and cable protection is not optional; it is essential. Approved circuit-breakers should be installed, as should correct weatherproof switches and plugs. Most things about garden railways are easygoing and subject to individual taste. Mains electricity is not one of these. Either you do it right or not at all if you want to live long and prosper!

To some people, this gives it a sense of prototypical purpose, which holds particularly true if you have an interest in correct timetable operation. The drawback is that it can often mean that you become involved in quite a lot of walking; with no time to sit and relax, watching the trains go by. My own railway overcomes this by having the two termini very close together, after the track has gone right around the boundaries of the garden. So I send my trains off and can enjoy the spectacle of them running as free spirits through my landscapes, and do not need to move until they arrive nearby at the end of their run.

**Out and Back**. With this layout there is a base area from where the train sets off. At some stage, there is a near-complete circle of track that turns the train round and heads it back from whence it came. Sometimes this includes a couple of points to offer the option of a complete circle so the trains can trundle round and round unattended without let or hindrance.

**Circuit**. This big circle of track, which may border the entire garden, seems to be the most common type of layout. It offers the best scope for carefree running – especially if you become a sociable operator who enjoys having plenty of visitors to run on your line. The problem is that, at some point, you may need to get inside the circle. This implies bridges and lift-out sections, or maybe something that can be stepped over. The circuit layout is particularly friendly towards steam and battery locomotives that are not radio controlled. The trains can roll ever onwards whilst you sit in a chair, sipping something long and cool. It is also the layout of choice for the high, elevated track where long passenger trains sweep round on a bare, almost stylized, setting. Here, it is the magnificence of the smoothly running, beautifully built, train that is the focus of the railway.

**Dog-Bone**. As its name suggests, this variation of the circuit layout is a long oval that has squashed-in sides. This forms a good area for a substantial station.

These three basic types of layout can be mixed together until there are tracks going off in all sorts of directions, with trains disappearing and then reappearing somewhere quite unexpected. Some people enjoy the pleasure of the garden railway as an object in its own right. This is subtly different to those who aim more for modelling prototype railways more accurately. Here, the arrangement of tracks is determined more by prototype practice and we are back in those realms of the difference between a garden railway and a model railway set in the garden.

Anomalies are certain to creep in when designing the track layout on paper. The most frequent mistake is having tracks too close together, particularly on curves where the 'throwover' of long bogie coaches extends the envelope of space they need. Sidings and passing loops are made far too short and, best of all, very sharp curves can be designed in. So, just like drawing outlines on the ground with that hosepipe for the overall shape of things, it makes sense to knock up a few cardboard cut-outs

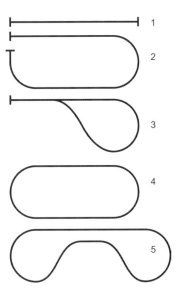

*The basic types of layout are: 1: End-to-end. 2: Nearly a circuit, with the two ends close together. 3: A return loop for out and back operation. 4: A complete circuit. 5: A dog-bone, which is a circuit with a squashed middle (a convenient location for a single station area).*

showing the plan of a typical commercial point as well as other items. In the scale I work in, a coach may be 2ft (60cm) long and it needs to run in a corridor of clearance that is 6in (15cm) wide. Out in the garden you can think *big* if you want to. The mental leap from the indoor H0/00 gauges (or even 0 gauge) that you have been used to can be quite a big one indeed.

I suggest that these practical points are the main factors in a successful garden railway. Only when the basics have been sorted out should you allow yourself to think about what sort of railway you want to build around them. A simple option would be to shop through the LGB catalogue and build a mid-European narrow-gauge railway that picks up the current for its electric motors from the track. You could use everything straight out of the box and the manufacturer will have thought out most of the technical details for you. I shall discuss options towards the end of the book but you may want to think of your personal preferences now. In my next reincarnation I should like my garden railway to be to 7mm scale 0 gauge and be of my

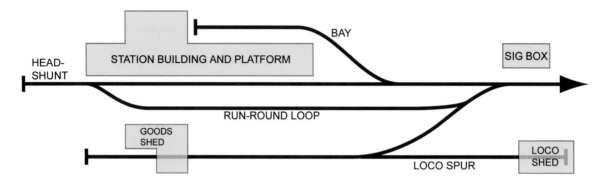

*The basic needs of a simple terminus include a run-round loop and maybe some simple engine stabling facilities.*

beloved Southern Region steam in Hampshire. Moreover, I would like to model something fairly accurately, such as features of the Gosport branch. But the narrow gauge of Compton Down is more than enough for this lifetime.

Maybe too, this is a good time to think again about how we think we will want to run the railway. If you are anticipating a very sociable scene, with plenty of groups running trains, then you will want to include space in the design for storing boxes and their owners. Your access needs will be different. More solitary people have only themselves to please. This overall process of planning is very much like a picture coming slowly into focus. It can be worth thinking about doing things in stages. Be happy to start with a fairly simple circuit that can be extended into a more ambitious form later. Despite all the planning, we may get something wrong. There is a strong argument for getting something running early on and using that as a starting point for more ambitious adventures in the light of experience.

That's it . . . we have planned as much as we can. It is time to do.

*Eventually those lines you draw on paper become a three-dimensional reality. Don't be afraid to amend your plans as you go along. The eye will often see something better when it has something tangible to work on.*

## LEGAL NICETIES

This is *not* a definitive guide to the law as it may affect garden railways: merely my own experience and observations of the do's and don'ts, bylaws, laws and common-sense things.

Electrical work in the garden has to be done correctly. Substantial electrical work on your property can be subject to inspection and you may be forced to have remedial work undertaken at your own expense.

When building a shed or outbuilding, you can erect one with a volume of up to a certain size without making an application for planning permission. Fortunately, the size allowed is generous enough to handle most ordinary garden railway needs, but do check. If you do have to apply for planning permission, take my tip and never call it a workshop. Call it a hobbies room instead.

There will be limitations on how close to a boundary wall you can erect a shed. However, in the back garden, with the agreement of your neighbour, you can probably keep a small portable shed next to the fence without offending anyone.

You are entitled to cut back any branches that have grown from a neighbour's garden into your own, but you must be prepared to return the cuttings (should this be requested!)

There are height restrictions for structures. Some local authorities are sterner than others when it comes to erecting a full-size signal in your garden without asking them first. When I had one, for the sake of a quiet life, I kept the top of the post to a level of 10ft (3m).

If you have groups of visitors, it is good manners, if nothing else, to make sure that their cars don't block the roads. I live by the side of a narrow lane and ask that visitors unload outside and then go to park in safe and unobtrusive locations.

Typically, a local authority may say that you can have up to four open days a year without things needing to be drawn to their attention. Life is simpler if visitors are by invitation only. However, if your area is having a day of open gardens for charity, then you can join in with that.

You are responsible for the safety of visitors on your property and these are litigious times. In reality this translates into a need for the reasonable care that you would want to employ anyway. Making a charge for entry to your property might well increase your responsibilities and it is not a friendly thing to do. However, a big open day might be the opportunity to pass a hat round for charity if you should feel so inclined.

Live steam needs to be treated with respect. Even small locomotives may need boiler certificates for use where public viewing is involved. The 16mm Association has a squadron of testers dotted about the country. They are often to be found at meetings and shows and may attend to your needs on the spot. There may also be a requirement for pressure testing gas tanks. You do not need certificates for private use. Larger, model-engineering type, live steam needs boiler certification. Very often, your local club will have access to a tester. Also, if the public is involved, there are some serious insurance implications to consider.

Although not strictly a legal requirement, perhaps this might be a suitable place to touch upon the delicate subject of how your railway might be disposed of after you have shuffled off this mortal coil. Don't rely on just chatting vaguely about it to relatives. Write it down somewhere. Very often the relevant scale association can help with disposal advice and prevent your loved ones from being ripped off. Could I add the personal observation, on this topic, that I think it is unfair to expect others to maintain your railway after you have gone. My suggestion is to let them know it is your wish that the railway is either sold complete for rebuilding elsewhere, or that it is dismantled joyfully and the proceeds of the sale passed on.

*As well as the concept of the two-dimensional plan, you will also start to get a feeling for the ephemeral way that three-dimensional spaces hang together. You may not be able to visualize them all in the planning stage, in which case they will come as a pleasant surprise when they materialize.*

# CHAPTER 3

# Foundations

The simplest foundation is just to lay some track on to the ground. Clip together a few lengths of pre-formed track (set-track) and you're in business! Great fun. As a child, I did just that with some tin-plate track, carefully ballasted with ashes, coal and soil (not received with unbridled parental joy). Thus, humbly, was the Compton Down railway born to a very small civil engineer. I laid it on some narrow concrete paths surrounding a pond, and in a rockery. Down at ground level, it seemed to reek of atmosphere to young eyes. I converted a clock-work engine into a narrow gauge outline and a love affair was started. To this day I remain an enthusiastic supporter of simple ephemeral railways as a starting point.

If I had laid the track on grass, I might have enjoyed a couple of days of pleasant running, with only a few bits of gunge going up into the mechanism but, very quickly, the rails would have been swallowed up by jungle. So it would make sense to form a barrier between the grass and the track. A neat shallow trench, lined with some sort of membrane (including old roofing felt) will do just that. Fill the trench with fine gravel and lay the track. This looks reasonable and will keep the grass back. There is also an aesthetic pleasure to be had from setting the sleepers into proper ballast and levelling it up in a prototypical manner.

The next stage is to raise the level of the track a few inches above the grass to stop it becoming contaminated with ground level dirt. The sides of the little trench could be lined with bits of old roofing slate before adding the membrane and a few natu-

*Having the track an inch or so above the grass stops the trackbed becoming invaded by grass. (Photo: courtesy* Die Gartenbahn)

*Low foundations, cast in concrete, will ensure that the railway runs smoothly through the rockery. (Photo: Phil Beckey)*

ral stones cemented outside the slates to hide them. Thus you have a low embankment and it all looks very pleasing. With a growing layout, the novelty of continually adjusting the track for level, in its ballast, can start to wear off. So how about concealing a long strip of pressure-treated (tanalized) wood under the stones with the track loosely pinned to it? The ballast then becomes merely cosmetic. By now we have reached the stage of having a length of flat and smoothly laid track running across the garden. We are making progress.

## HIGHER AMBITIONS

For a variety of reasons, you may want to build a bit higher. It could be that the ground slopes anyway and we want to maintain a level. Perhaps more height is wanted to make operation easier, and to give the trains more visual impact. So you could build a double row of walls. The easiest to build are those using natural stone, rendered with a little cement. Brick walls are neater but only when they are well laid. For economy, concrete blocks could be used but these need disguising behind low evergreenery of some sort. These low walls may well help to make gardening easier. If there are rigid boundaries between grass, flowerbeds and railways, there is a sort of self-imposed neatness.

Cuttings need to be approached with caution if we don't want them to become ponds, compost

*A combination of barriers helps to separate plant life, pond and railway.*

*A simple trough, made up of loose stones concreted in place, will hold loose ballast neatly in place and present a pleasing appearance. Note the radio transmitter. You can be sure that the receiving gubbins is secreted away in that van.*

heaps or litter bins. So the underlying trench needs to have a slope on it that allows water to run away. It is a good idea to line the sides of cuttings with something like natural stones, rather than have badly behaved loose soil or grass. Alternatively we could plant some fast-growing ground cover early on to stabilize things. Casting concrete against a mould made of a rubber car mat can form a rather natty retaining wall. At this stage I will draw your attention to Rowlands Mix – named after the eponymous Dave who blessed us with it. It is sand, cement and peat (or a more ecologically friendly substitute these days). This is not particularly strong and so is ideal for insetting track. But what it does is to really encourage mosses and the like to grow quickly and hide the rawness of the concrete. Within a few years the track can become just a couple of bruised lines through a green carpet.

Having an interest in garden railways doesn't mean that we have to be horny-handed sons or daughters of toil. Those hands can be quite soft and delicate if we are office workers and the like. If this is your first major experience of chucking concrete about, it pays to look after the hands. I can't get on with using builders' gloves. The trick is to put some moisturising cream on before, as well as after. Even just rubbing a little olive oil into the skin beforehand can make a difference. Similarly, it seems poor strategy to pull a muscle or risk a back injury. I take very good care to cherish myself at all times with a dedicated programme of self-restraint.

Concrete and stone can also be softened in appearance by the application of organic matter by another route. Paint some white glue on and then jabble (dab) in yoghurt, stale milk, cowpats, sheep-droppings or any permutation of these. This is a frankly disgusting procedure but it works.

*A slightly higher pair of rough stone walls will take the railway further off the ground and be more comfortable to use.*

*A typical mould, built by Phil Beckey for casting a concrete viaduct, is merged into an existing low embankment. (Photo: Phil Beckey)*

*A fully fledged, waist-high retaining wall is built of rough natural stones. On a wet day it has a lovely colour and patina. You really don't want to know why there is a loco firebox and boiler set into the wall!*

## TERRAFORMING

*The retaining walls do not have to be uniformly level. With a bit of imagination they can flow up and down, creating interest to the trackbed.*

Finally you can throw all restraint to the wind and build waist-high stone (or brick) baseboards. All thought of blending your railway down into the ground has been abandoned. The raised structures strike boldly across the garden. But perhaps, even in this case, the garden itself can be enhanced. Those baseboards can be widened to incorporate areas of raised garden where maintenance is easy (although outside the scope of this book, such garden design is kind to wheelchair users). Indeed, I will go further. Why not really feature the vertical element in the garden? Be bold and break away from those very flat two dimensions. The garden can be formed into hills and valleys, and look more dramatic for it. Make use of that height by landscaping the fronts of walls as rock faces planted with tiny greenery. The whole thing will make a more dramatic setting for the railway. Although I have never tried it out, a scheme that sounds very promising involves building a big 'island' in the middle of the garden: a giant rockery perhaps 10ft (3m) high with the railway running around it. A radical refinement would be to build a garden shed *inside* this man-made mountain. Give it a transparent roof. No one says that you have to be conventional: it isn't compulsory.

*This simple drift mine, roughly 6ft (1.8m) above ground level, is an example of where the foundations have become part of the terraforming.*

*Conventional concrete blocks can be used for retaining walls. They could be hidden by small bushes with time, but an alternative is to make them bright and bold with masonry paint.*

## BRICKS

There's quite a lot more to a brick than meets the eye. As well as the modern, rather characterless examples that dominate the scene, there is a world of old mellow regional bricks to be appreciated. To some of us, a brick wall can be a particularly satisfying addition to the garden. But if you need to use modern bricks, ask for 'rustic-faced': they have a slightly more interesting texture to them. To economize, you can ask for seconds or regrades. These are quite strong enough for garden use and often have an interesting uneven finish to them that looks quite attractive in a low wall.

Real economy comes where someone gives you a pile of old bricks that still have the mortar sticking to them. Cleaning them up by chipping away at them can be a monotonous procedure, but tell yourself that they are free and this eases the pain. I suppose I shouldn't say this but, for low decorative walls, you don't have to clear the mortar off perfectly. You can still build a neat brick wall by bedding slightly knobbly bricks into fresh mortar. When you have cleaned up the joints it can still look tidy, although not as strong as a properly laid wall. But then, it doesn't have to support anything structural. If your bricks still have old mortar filling the frog (recess), the wall may be much less well bonded, but plastering it up with a rough layer of mortar on the inside face will restore some of that strength.

*Neat brickwork has an appeal all of its own. If you can do the preparatory work yourself, getting a bricklayer in to make a really good job of it might not be too much of a luxury. (Photo: Phil Beckey)*

This is not the place for a course in bricklaying – it's something you can read up on if it's new to you. Perfection is not required – provided the courses of a wall look reasonably level, any cement smears and slight irregularities can be nicely hidden under a coat of masonry paint. Indeed, the use of a bold colour on painted brick walls can often give the garden a real 'lift'. Given a choice, it is better to avoid white on low walls. It becomes discoloured so easily by dirt splashed up by the rain.

But however large or small your raised stone structures are, remember that they represent space that can be used. A short area of projecting wall can be covered with several strips of timber to form a garden seat. Chambers can be built into raised structures for storage. Perhaps the neatest way of doing this is to set a plastic storage box, on its side, into the stone or brick wall whilst it is being built. Large openings and recesses will need a joist of some sort to support any weight above. A portion of angled steel bed frame, appropriately painted, is useful and a prime case for keeping an eye open for suitable scrap. For a deep recess, the top could be lined with a few short lengths of scaffolding tube.

## NOBODY KNOWS THE RUBBLE I'VE SEEN (OLD NEGRO SPIRITUAL)

Whilst you are building the concrete and rubble structures, it may be worth considering sculpting in any rock faces you have planned at the same time. This helps to get a more natural, blended look. Where possible, do try to have a look at the real thing for guidance.

The following photographs include a section of rock face that is also blended into the landscape surrounding the track. It represents sloping beds of sandstone. To get this effect I have a background layer of old stones or pieces of broken up concrete, popped in place roughly, but with an eye to that diagonal bedding. A 6:1 mix of sand and cement, that isn't too wet, is flung off the trowel with a flick of the wrist so that it splatters against the rubble. This is then brushed over with a very wet and wide brush to bed it down. The brush strokes follow the line of the bedding. One or two bits of detail are

*Looser bricklaying can be quite satisfactory with older bricks of character. Low walls also present an opportunity to incorporate any interesting cast iron or stone items you may have.*

then shaped with a flat stick. The job is left to stiffen up for a few hours and then the bristles of a yard brush are swiftly and lightly dragged across the mix, in the direction of the bedding. It was at this stage that the photo was taken. Everything will be left to harden for a couple of days and then the surplus loose sand brushed off.

## A COMPLEX EXAMPLE IN STONE AND CONCRETE

Let us put some of these thoughts together in one intricate example, which will illustrate many of these points. Working on the principle that complicated is merely lots of simples put together, we will have a look at a part-built complex that has various

*What a mess! Tracks will be curving and dipping in all sorts of ways. Establishing flat datum levels gives something that the intricate geometry can spring from. That steel joist across the front will support yet another track, at a higher level, when the main lines have been laid.*

levels and gradients, some of which are curved, and where tracks intertwine. The secret is to start with fixed reference points. So a plain block wall is built at the back and a flat concrete base is laid. It may be useful to draw a few lines in paint to indicate levels and directions. Working outwards and upwards from the back, start adding the bulk to this terraforming. Rough retaining walls can be built out of old bricks and cement. Then the spaces behind can be filled up with rubble. Do not be tempted to use turf or soil as a fill material. It settles over the years and this can contribute to subsidence in even apparently rigid concrete decks above.

You can mark lines and offsets as a guide to gradients or there is the simpler route of running some taut string at the inclination required and then standing well back from the job and lining it up by eye as you go. The basic core of a rising embankment can be made of bricks. Thereafter the level can be finalized with a concrete mix, trowelled on. This is finished off with the traditional long straight edge that is shuffled from side to side, smoothing off the excess and revealing any hollows you may have left.

Whilst all this major shaping is being done, don't forget to leave plenty of voids for future plantings.

*The underground caverns and tunnels were built fairly early on, of course. Clearances are generous. Fine-scale modelling is all very well, but not worth skinned knuckles.*

When the time comes, put a bit of gravel in the bottom and then some organic matter to provide nutrients and to hold moisture. If you have a pond, the sludge from the bottom and any excess weed or algae will do very nicely for this. If you then use bagged growing mixture, add a little gravel or sharp sand just to open it up a bit, unless a specific plant calls for something else. As soon as I have finished creating these pockets, I stain any concrete around them and then plant them up immediately. That way, the growing process has started early and will continue whilst you build the rest of the layout.

With an intricate site like this, it is even more important not to build in inaccessibility. Plan for safe places to put your feet when a train stalls right at the back of the area. It also makes sense to lay track at those back areas at this early stage. It is better to do it in comfort now than in backbreaking discomfort later. As can be seen in the photographs, the landscape at the very back was complete and the track laid. The next step was to lay the track for the underground mine workings and build rough brick walls adjacent to them. The tunnels were then formed, complete with natural rock faces and retaining walls. Paving slabs were laid over the tunnels and then a complete concrete deck cast on top. This gave a new level to work from.

A second gradient was built, and track laid. This is the one with the train on it. A steel joist was placed in front of this concrete deck to take more stone walling that raised a further, higher, level not shown in the photographs. As this area progresses there are many intricate cross channels to be installed for various reasons (such as spaces to run the wiring of a set of outdoor white Christmas tree lights, which make for extremely cheap, low-voltage illumination). If you are very good at computer design, you may well be able to draw all of this out in advance, in three dimensions that can be rotated. I can't. So I doodle things as best I can on paper and then paint outlines on flat concrete surfaces. There is a need to watch out for any traps like overly sharp curves, tracks that are squeezed too close together, or impossible gradients.

*Although no detail has been installed yet, there is already a sense of the dark and mysterious from these underground foundations.*

*An interesting way of fairing new concrete over old is to carve false edging stones when the material is still fairly soft. A stiff brush also adds a bit of texture.*

## LEGS AND TOPS

Drive a couple of short wooden stakes into the ground and then nail a plank on top to join them. This is a simple railway foundation. If some track is pinned on top, our trains can run smoothly backwards and forwards. Although this will be adequate for a couple of weeks in summer, shortcomings will soon become apparent. Wood 'moves' for a pastime. It also rots when stuck into wet earth. A simple alternative is to stick the uprights into ice-cream tubs filled with concrete and then set these into holes in the ground. Angle the cement upwards and slightly towards the post, so that rainwater runs away. It costs so little extra to get your timber order pressure treated by the timber yard that it is worth doing anyway. You will recoup the cost many times over through needing less preservative in the coming years.

Don't be tempted to skimp on those uprights. For low-level baseboards, make those uprights 2×2in (5×5cm) – perhaps in pairs – and for waist-level track, use at least 3×3in (7×7cm). There is no need to order planed timber – sawn is fine. Neither do you need to buy expensive hardwood. This may be controversial, but, in my experience, softwood is preferable for use out of doors, provided you plan to keep an eye on it. It also absorbs preservative much better. Excluding water from the pores of the wood prevents rot. Some hardwoods contain natural substances that resist rot, but there is a time limit. However, there is no need to be dogmatic about this – if you happen to have a nice stash of hardwood around the place that is just begging to be used, then do so. Old, well-seasoned timber is an advantage if it is available. Builders' planks have always been highly regarded. Some timber yards specialize in wood that is so green that I swear it sprouts in spring. A useful tip: don't just ask for so many lengths from your supplier. Pick them out individually yourself. That way you make sure that you avoid the warped and twisted bits that the yard is anxious to get rid of. For the decking itself, I like to go for overkill and use lengths of 4×2in (10× 5cm) treated softwood, side by side, with cross-bracing underneath. Under no circumstances use chipboard or MDF out of doors – it will only end in tears. So what about plywood? To be blunt, I hate

*Well-built brick pillars will support a substantial deck for a large terminus area.*

the stuff being used for trackbeds. It sags, warps, twists and delaminates in time. It takes longer to deform with marine ply and/or by protecting it but it will eventually cause problems. I think we should compare notes about time here. It may seem rather odd to worry about how things will look in fifteen years time but if you have children you will know all about the problem. You look at a toddler, blink twice, and then all six feet of him is coming home from the pub with his mates.

If you must use plywood, make it thick and exterior quality – marine ply preferably. One useful budget option is to ask for shuttering ply. This is thick and fairly durable but is smooth on one face only. It is quite a bit cheaper than other forms of outdoor plywood. Again, it pays to select your own sheets from the yard and sign them to make sure that these are what gets delivered. When you have cut out the sections and shapes, char all the edges with a blowlamp. Whilst the wood is still warm, paint with undiluted, waterproof white glue and paint the flat surfaces with dilute glue. Brace the undersides with reinforcing timber.

*Brian Spring built neat timber foundations for his track. The raised arch features a lift-up section. In due course, a row of low shrubs will hide much of his woodworking.*

*Very elegant legs, made from plastic drainpipes, support neat decking on this gauge 1 layout. It is spacious and airy underneath for easy mowing and strimming. (Photo: Geoff Culver)*

Whatever the decking, it is a good idea to coat the top in a black mastic sealant and then pin down heavy-grade roofing felt, wrapping it around the edges, much as you would a shed roof. This has the added advantage of giving a realistic, textured surface on which to build your railway. There is an argument that when pins are driven down through the felt, they let in water that is trapped underneath, which rots the wood. My own experience is that provided the mastic layer is fairly thick, any holes tend to be self-sealing. Facing off the edge of baseboards with 6×1in (15×2.5cm) softwood makes a neat job and provides additional support against sagging.

I know I seem to be labouring these points. You are bursting to run trains and I am burbling on about all this. But getting the foundations right can make the difference between heaven and hell during the coming years!

> Skimping on the building of timber bases has caused quite a few problems, but recorded history has shown that building them too strongly has thrown up few problems thus far.

There are some good alternatives to timber, particularly for the upright legs. PVC drainpipes are excellent. If the square section is used, those flat surfaces are easier to bolt things to. If you don't like the appearance of shiny plastic, there is a useful dodge. Go over it with sandpaper. This will give it a lighter, matt finish. Get a sample pot of olive-coloured, acrylic bathroom paint and rub it into the roughened surface with a cloth. This will give an instant, mellow patina of age. Another alternative for uprights is to use old scaffolding pipe if you have access to a source. But whatever you use, be aware that the ground you drive them into will probably not remain stable over time.

There are commercial bases available for wooden fence posts. They are either deep spiky things or have flat plates at the bottom for bolting into concrete. These have been employed by some garden railway builders to good effect and may be worth investigating. Likewise, there are proprietary gadgets for securing timber beams to others at various forms of right angle. A browse through a large DIY store for ideas could be useful.

> Thinking in terms of many years' service out of doors, avoid the temptation to use plastic-coated steel for foundations. Once the plastic starts to crack, moisture gets in underneath and it is ridiculously hard work trying to remove the plastic coating to get at the metal. Quite often, by the time you notice the plastic starting to flake, the metal is well corroded anyway.

It is a good idea to incorporate some sort of height adjustment when the time comes to fit the decking on to the uprights: something involving T pieces, long bolts and some spacer washers sounds good. However, there are many ingenious alternatives and the chances are that the one you come up with will work splendidly. But they should not involve steel nuts and bolts. Indeed, raw steel is best avoided in the garden wherever possible and although we can slow the oxidation process down by all manner of paints, oil and grease, it will eventually go rusty. There are some applications where it cannot be avoided, but ordinary steel fixings will inevitably come back to haunt you. Plated screws will take longer to start rusting but they too will eventually start to feel the effects of the passing wet years. Big chunky nuts and bolts will be made of steel, but they are so thick that they will long outlast you. The main precaution to take is to grease the thread before screwing the nuts on, just in case you need to undo them years hence. One of the sillier questions asked about a garden railway is 'What happens if it rains?' It is a nice feeling to be able to give a smug smile and say, 'It just gets wet.'

Wider timber decking can also be supported on brick piers or even stone foundations. You may well

*One good method for height adjustment is to use screw-feet at the bottom of timber uprights.*

find, depending on the slope and layout of the garden, that a mixture of foundation techniques will be called for. I have one terminus that is fitted against the wall of my house. It would have been a *very* bad idea to build a solid stone structure there as it would have bridged the damp course, so a conventional timber deck was used.

Alternatively, black reconstituted plastic is an excellent material for outdoor use. You may well need to track down a supplier on the Internet or in trade directories. UPVC section, such as is used for house bargeboards or windowsills associated with double-glazing, is a superbly durable material. Its main drawback is that it is *very* white! If you want to paint it, give it a wash with hot soapy water first, to remove any residual traces of anti-stick surface compound. Then go over it with medium sandpaper to roughen the surface slightly. It is expensive to buy new, but offcuts from jobs are not unknown.

## BRACKETS

A final option to be considered for supports is to use brackets that spring from existing upright structures, provided they are suitable. If you would like to run a shelf along the side of an existing brick or block wall, then it is a straightforward drill, plug and screw job. Regard timber fences with suspicion. The upright posts are only as good as the concrete foundations they are placed in. Anything less is not likely to withstand a decent gale. Never, under any circumstances, drill into a concrete fence post. It will let moisture into the steel reinforcing bar inside. This rust will expand and burst the concrete open ('concrete sickness').

You may well succumb, as I have in the past, to the temptation of using those grey-painted, pressed-steel brackets so beloved of hardware stores. They are so cheap and convenient that you

*My complex garden railway once sat around a neat lawn. The windmill is not compulsory.*

tell yourself that they won't rust through in ten years – which they will. If you must use them, give them a couple of coats of black bitumastic paint before fitting in place. This can slow down the ravages of time.

## INTEGRATED FOUNDATIONS

In an integrated garden, there are other foundations to think about. This would be the time to build rockeries, for example. The majority of the hump can be made of builders' rubble or used as somewhere to bury something chunky and awkward. Somewhere, there is a cracked engine block off a Ford Mustang under my landscape – but that's another story. This rubble will provide free drainage. Topsoil and big lumps of rock go over the hump and look nice. There are books galore on how to lay paths and patios on sand, so I needn't go into that here. Concrete areas of hardstanding may be worth considering. Building the foundations of a garden railway can be – it has to be admitted – hard work. If you can plan your activities in such a way as to avoid having to move material twice, you will be happier.

If the planning has been thought through, you can get round undertaking a vast amount of heavy labour before being able to lay even an inch of track. There is nothing in the rules that says it *has* to be all done at once, which is another good reason why you might think about building a small area first, just to get the feel of things. Getting a train running somewhere, somehow, fairly early on is important. It also helps to spread the cost of construction over a couple of years. A few wagons sitting on a length of track is a tremendous spur to further things. Allow yourself this luxury early on and find true happiness.

# CHAPTER 4

# Track

Now that there is a decent foundation in place, you can get down to serious railway business. It is time to consider track, concentrating on the garden gauges to start with. Let's start right down at toy level. Even all-plastic toy track has its uses. It can

be put to its intended use of being a temporary clip-together system upon which we can run battery-powered engines, hauling light wagons. It is rather thin and floppy so needs to be laid on a rigid flat surface. The plastic may well be of the soft soapy type that paints peel off for a pastime. Thus if it is bright red you are more of less stuck with it. Hopefully, it will be moulded in black and be less obtrusive. One advantage of these softer types of plastic is that they are surprisingly durable out of doors, resisting the attempts of ultraviolet light to make them brittle.

Tinplate track, beloved of my youth, is equally usable in a light-hearted way. However, despite the tin coating, it rusts out of doors. Train collectors may get a bit upset at what they see as vandalism, but I take the view that it was meant to be played with. This track, like the all-plastic stuff, suffers from having toy-like, very sharp curves. This is slightly less of a problem if we are going to run short engines and wagons. Occasionally a variant of tinplate track may be encountered. The rails are folded round in thin metal and then pressed into slots cut in wood sleepers, which gives a flexible track that looks reasonable from a distance. Like traditional tinplate track, because it has a rounded

top, it may be less tolerant of fine wheel profiles. I am not convinced of its durability and strength over the years, and so would resist the temptation to buy quantities of it because it was cheap. Some experience has shown that the rails have a tendency to pop out of the slots, but it has had its advocates. Finally, in this group, there is a cast alloy sectional track made by Mamod. This is relatively expensive per length but once screwed down on a rigid base, it seems to be extremely weather resistant. The only drawback is that the cast alloy connecting lugs are prone to snapping off with careless handling.

## THE MOST POPULAR TRACKS

But now we turn to the largest single group of track systems. It features non-rusting rails, slotted into plastic sleepers. For simplicity of use and sheer durability, LGB is highly regarded. Its strength has been demonstrated by having an elephant walking on it – a *most* unsuitable animal to keep in your garden, I would have thought. It is to 45mm gauge and intended for two-rail electrification. Part of its strength comes from the fact that it is over scale, and so it is crude to look at if you have ambitions for realistic modelling. But this is less of a problem in the overall vista of a garden. The set track curves and some of the points are very sharply angled but it has to be said, this track is very popular because of its extreme simplicity of laying and durability thereafter. Lengths of flexible track (flexitrack) are available and they offer much more realism. They are, as their name suggests, capable of being bent flexibly into large-radius reverse curves. Because LGB is a complete system in its own right, information about laying the track and wiring it is freely available with the product. It is simple to use and has extra inherent strength in its own right. This means that it is more tolerant of poor foundations. There are a number of smaller companies who make track products that are roughly compatible and there are always new players coming into the market. It isn't for me to offer value judgements of one against another, but I make the observation that it is probably better for a newcomer to work with one established system.

Peco produces a flexible track system in a variety of scales and gauges that are extremely useful in many applications. It is more attractive and many people have found it to be eminently practical. It likes to have decent foundations but otherwise it has thrown up few problems over the years. In its early days, the plastic had a tendency to go brittle, especially if it got creosote on it (now no longer available), but it has proved useful to many nonetheless, including me. Compared to the sheer bulk of G-scale track, 0-gauge fine-scale track seems slender and delicate – and hence looks nice. But this does mean extra care in handling the track lengths if you are new to them. It also means that track foundations need to be truer and stronger. A coarse track like LGB has a certain amount of inherent rigidity but finer-scale systems are more floppy. The fine-tipped ends of point blades are fitted to a sliding tierod that moves them from side to side. Those of some finer-scale systems, like Peco, are apt to come adrift after prolonged pounding by heavy steam locos, so wise people take the precaution of soldering an extra-strong tierod in place before laying track.

Then, of course, there are the dreadnought traditional track systems – Bonds, Milbro, Bassett-Lowke and Leeds are names you might encounter. Years ago, trains rode upon tracks where chunky rails were slotted into cast white-metal chairs, which then pinned on to correct wood sleepers, which were sometimes pinned to strengthening battens underneath. Building this track was a relaxing way to get sore fingers. The end result was a bit crude and over scale for fine-scale standard gauge trains. But when the big explosion of interest in narrow gauge came along they enjoyed a newfound popularity. Because of the durability of this sort of track, it is possible that you may come across second-hand examples from time to time. I have several small sections of it on my railway that are now over one hundred years old.

A modern variant of this is where small plastic chairs, with moulded spigots underneath, plug into plastic or wood sleepers that have holes predrilled to gauge. These are prone to 'unplug' with heavy use and time. However, a couple of fine pins, such

*Peco 0-gauge fine-scale track bedded down in ballast. A strip of wood with some notches cut in ensures consistent, perfect spacing between the tracks as they are laid. (Photo: Phil Beckey)*

*When that neat track is surrounded by nature, it has an attraction all of its own. (Photo: Phil Beckey)*

as veneer pins, every fourth sleeper or so, deals with that. Another option is to use rails that are directly soldered to printed circuit board (PCB) sleepers. These don't seem to have the strength of other track systems if subjected to heavy punishment by trains – particularly narrow gauge – but, again, there are examples of this system being used successfully in the garden. This isn't a subject of absolutes; it is all relative.

*Plastic plug-in chairs by Tenmille are pushed into jig-drilled holes in wood sleepers. In this case, they are set in concrete. The overall brown-ness of track is mostly proportional to the amount of braking done. Thus tracks tend to be browner on track that is approaching a station, or where a lot of shunting is done.*

---

### MISCELLANEA

For the sake of completeness perhaps I should say that the above brief overview does not include the many odds and ends that people have experimented with over the years. In more cash-strapped times, rails of round fence wire were employed. There have been wooden rails, all sorts of small steel section – anything in fact, which was obtainable free.

If you think you have invented a reliable working system of your own, then give it a try. I have a particular fascination for plateway track, whereby the L-shaped rails guide wheels that are just plain discs. There is a whole world of innovation out there just waiting to be explored if you are so minded.

## RAIL TYPES

Folk like to argue about all sorts of things. I weep for the trees that were cut down to make the paper upon which have been printed the arguments for and against different rail materials. I prefer brass because it dulls down to a natural looking brown colour with time and it is easy to cut, file and solder. Some of my rail is extremely old and yet it will outlive me by generations. There are those who like to see a shiny polished steel rail and choose either stainless steel or aluminium. They may well be right. I find stainless steel rail rather hard work to file if I am making points, and I have noticed that some aluminium rail goes a bit powdery. But both give good service. I make the observation that steel rail rusts. If it becomes pitted, it makes for rougher running. In extreme examples, like early Lima track that had very fine section rail, it eventually disappears altogether leaving nothing more than a double row of rust stains! Old catalogues used to speak of 'sheradized' steel. This was plated with a rust-resistant surface. But running trains would wear this through on the tops and then rust would set in. My preference is to keep lengths of steel rail in realistic scenic piles along the side of the line. However, it is generally accepted that nickel silver is the most widely used material for rails. This looks more of a steel colour, is easy to work and takes solder well. It is extensively used commercially and I commend it to your soul.

For the complete newcomer, let me pause a moment and point out that there are two types of rail section in use: bullhead and flat-bottomed. Bullhead rail has a base that is the same shape as its top (originally thought of as an economy measure whereby worn rail could be re-used by turning it upside down. It didn't really work!). This sits in chairs that have profiled jaws to take it. Flat-bottomed rail is what its name suggests. I mention this now because the rail joiners (hereinafter referred to as fishplates) are different, and a bit of fiddling is needed to join one type of rail to the other. Rail heights can vary too. They will be referred to in thousandths of an inch. For instance, 'Code 200' rail is 200 thousandths of an inch high. Once again, it takes a bit of fancy footwork for a beginner to connect rails of different heights. So we come back again to the advice that it is better to stick to one make of track if possible. Everything is nicely compatible and all is well with the world. But you have to be realistic about this. If someone offers to give you fifty yards of a different type of track to your own, then by all means take it.

Naturally, we have been concentrating primarily on tracks for those garden gauges, all of which are dear to my heart. But there are whole other worlds out there to conquer. Given the use of nickel silver or brass rail, we can use commercial systems in smaller scales out of doors quite happily. Freely available H0/00-gauge systems work well, given fairly flat and durable foundations. Larger-scale models of narrow gauge prototypes can run on it. On a small layout I have like this, I use battery power and the points are not electrically operated. This is to make for a railway that is maintenance free: important because it is only a modest diversion from my larger-scale empire.

## LAYING THE TRACK

Time, I think, to get a flavour of laying a bit of flexible track. Given a plank of wood as a base, laying

*Track laying in its simplest form: pinned down to a board through roofing felt. If there is a good coat of mastic under the felt, any holes tend to be self-sealing. Steel pins generally grip better than brass ones over the decades.*

a straight run of flexible track is straightforward, but there are one or two useful short cuts. First, the straight bits need to be straight and so a straight edge to line things up is useful. I find a lot of employment for a metre-long aluminium ruler around the garden railway, and this is what I reach for first. Starting at one end, pin the track down. Use fine pins at both ends of the sleepers, not a big nail in the middle (this can make the track buckle inwards). Pin the ends of every fourth sleeper or thereabouts. There is an ongoing argument as to whether brass or steel pins are better. Brass does not rust but steel grips better over a long period of time. I am happiest when using 18mm steel veneer pins. But it isn't obligatory. However, where pins are involved, you won't be surprised to learn that a proper pin hammer makes life easier. If you have access to a grinder, one useful tip is to grind the

tang at the back of the hammer head until a small pointed tip forms of about 4mm square. This makes for a lovely delicate little hammer that will find plenty of employment.

With a length of flexible track now pinned down in a straight line, we have to consider joining it to another piece. You will see that the sleepers of the first length are evenly spaced because webs tie them together. For the sake of neat track laying, we want to maintain that even spacing. It is helpful to cut a small piece of wood that drops between the sleepers of a piece of track, inside the rails. This then acts as a template to make sure that the first sleeper of the second length is nicely positioned. Incidentally, if you need to slide rail along that plastic web moulding, give the track a quick spray of WD-40 first. It makes it easier. But before we start to pin down that second length, we need to fit fishplates.

*Dave Lomas has properly 'inset' the track in concrete inside his well-detailed loco shed. He took good care to ensure that the grooves were kept well clear, to help smooth running. (Photo: Michael O'Hara)*

*For seekers of atmosphere, it is worthwhile keeping a large photo or two of real track in prominent view.*

They should be a tight fit and be just a bit difficult to slide on to rail ends. You will find that fine-nosed pliers are useful. Indeed, never go into the garden without them as they always come in handy.

Curves with a large radius are most easily set out with a bit of chalk on the end of a long piece of string. I would also make the point that long and gentle reverse curves have a more natural appearance than long runs of determinedly straight track. It somehow makes the railway look bigger.

So, keeping the track true and stable, continue to tap the little pins in. As soon as the first two lengths of track are laid, you will need to test them for smooth running. Run a wagon or two up and down to check that it goes across the rail joint smoothly.

While pinning down straight track is fairly easy, laying down flexitrack can be more problematic, as the rail on the inside of the curve is going to stick out far too long and/or the rail on the outside of the curve will be too short. So this is a good time to learn how to cut rail. Depending on your chosen scale, it may be possible to get various cropping gadgets and jigs. But, used properly, a junior hacksaw will do nicely, given a sharp, fine-toothed blade. The rail needs to be cut off as square as possible and without any ragged bits. The easiest way to achieve this at first is to saw a fraction over length and then just touch the ends with a file. It is particularly important that there

are no burrs on the bottom web of the rail or else you may have trouble getting fishplates on. If you can cut the rail away from the site, held in a vice, a useful trick is to put the rail in upside-down so that the cleanest part of the cut is where you need it. If the rail has to be cut on site, the big difficulty is holding the track still whilst doing so. The easiest way of achieving this is to use an offcut of wood with a couple of wide grooves sawn in that will slip over the railtops. Press down on the wood, gently saw with a junior hacksaw and the job is done.

## A NATURAL FLUIDITY

Flexible track has the advantage that it can sweep in gentle sinuous curves across a landscape, rather than give that slightly toy-like look that comes from just clipping straights and curves together. Part of this is because the full-size railway uses transition curves. The best way of describing this is that the straight track slowly evolves into a curve. There is a natural fluidity to everything. If flexible track is to be bent to a very sharp radius, it is better to pull the rails out of the sleeper web and pre-bend them. It makes the curves smoother and avoids those dog-legs that tend to creep in at rail joints. You can buy small adjustable roller tool gadgets for this quite cheaply.

The slight tilt of track on high-speed curves is known as superelevation. However, the transition from flat to slightly tilted needs to be very gradual. If not, long wheel-based wagons or locomotives will try to climb over the higher track and derail. If you are aiming to build a narrow gauge or a rural standard gauge railway, then aim to keep things as flat as possible.

## YOU'VE GOT A POINT THERE

Ready-made points are easy to lay, but you must make sure that they are truly flat and not pinned down one side too tightly. The most usual cause of derailments at points comes from wheels that want to clamber over the railtops and try to escape. Making sure things are flat avoids most of the dangers. If our railway is going to use two-rail electrification there may be some wiring considerations to think about, but I will look at these in a later chapter. For now, there is just the point lever to consider. Out in the garden, this is usually a simple accessory that can be bought over the counter. To connect it to the point itself, one or two purpose-made fittings are available, but I am rather fond of using model aeroplane control rods fitted with nylon clevises on the ends. Don't forget that narrow gauge rolling stock can be wider than you think. There are those of us who have fitted a lever to a point, only to find that the first train that passes it doesn't actually do so! For remote control, there is an interest in compressed air lines but these systems are outside my experience. They come as bolt-together assemblies with easy-to-follow instructions and it has to be said that they look very impressive in operation. However, you are more likely to encounter low-voltage electric point motors.

The final topic on track laying is more about aesthetics than practicality. I believe that it is worthwhile making things look right as well as work well. For example, if you have two tracks, side by side, going round a long curve, make sure that the curve is even and that the distance between the tracks remains the same. For this sort of thing, there are plenty of little home-made jigs you can put together. Typically, you could make a long radius rod out of a strip of timber and pin a couple of

wood blocks underneath that would drop between the rails. Thus you start your curve on both tracks, and then fight it round a bit at a time. The perfection of line is a pleasure to see and, of course, makes smooth running.

## HUMPTY-BUMPTY

There is an alternative possible strategy for narrow gauge railways, one that needs a little bit of courage. You can deliberately break some of the rules but in a controlled way. If track is being lightly set into a concrete base with everything smoothed in together, you can break away from the flat look. A run of plain track can have gentle undulations introduced. They need to be thought out so that short ups are followed by short downs. This avoids the operational difficulties of gradients by letting the train's momentum carry it over the small humps and dips. If this is combined with equally gentle reverse curves, the three-dimensional end result can be as appealing, in its own way, as that magnificently engineered main line for standard gauge trains.

When laying track, it makes sense to install any conduit for wiring at the same time. On a large two-rail layout, you might consider laying a full run of cable alongside the track right at the start: something that will act as the main circuit for you to branch off from later. Incidentally, if you have a circuit of two-rail track, it makes sense to have a deliberate break in it – with plastic fishplates – somewhere. It is bridged with a loop of wire and a switch. If a train suddenly stops on a circuit, you can pinpoint the source of a fault without being confused by current coming round the other way.

## LOOSE BALLASTING

So far I have talked about laying track on timber bases. There is a traditional alternative that invites us to emulate the real thing and lay it loose in ballast. Chicken grit is a favourite for this, but there is the problem of the scale effect to be overcome. Our model track is featherweight and, in loose ballast, easily disturbed. This can be resolved by pinning it

*Peco 16mm track set in fine gravel that is bonded in white glue. Long thin oil stains tend to occur where engines are working hard uphill. In stabling areas, oil gets everywhere.*

on to treated wood battens that are hidden under the tiny stones. However, there are many advocates of loose ballast. They like the appearance and the traditional nature of it. There is a real aesthetic pleasure to be had from laying track in the proto-typical manner and then coming along with tiny tools and brushes, to get beautifully graded ballast with straight bevelled edges. However, re-doing the job for the umpteenth time in a month because it has rained heavily or next door's cat has run amok can lead to tears! It is possible to glue the ballast in place. If you use waterproof PVA glue for this pur-pose, buy it in 5-litre tubs from a discount supplier, rather than in tiny tubes from a model shop: the process of bankruptcy is such a painful one . . . .

Ballast that has been contaminated with soil and dirt will provide a happy home for weeds of any sort, so try to keep it clean. A useful option is for unobtrusive barriers to be put down at the sides of ballast areas. A good example would be the corru-gated metal lawn edging, driven down until it is flush with the ground. A home-made weed-killing wagon can be run in future years to keep things as they should be. Incidentally, that same wagon can be used to dribble preservative on to wooden sleep-ers. But for the less romantically minded amongst us, a watering can with the rose slightly hooded by a piece of plastic tube is much quicker.

This may sound rather drastic but I like to bed my track in cement. I generally use a 6:1 mix of sharp sand and cement. Should I need to make any

changes, this taps out fairly cleanly with a pin ham-mer and an old screwdriver used as a chisel. I build my basic stone and concrete foundations, with the approximate trackbed level, first. Then I prop the track in place with little pieces of slate, and flood in a weak mix. Just as the mix has started to go off, but before it becomes hard (a bit like cheese in consis-tency), I whistle over it with a wire brush and this blends everything in beautifully, whilst making sure that the tops and insides of the rails are perfectly clean. Needless to say, concreting points solid is not a terribly good idea.

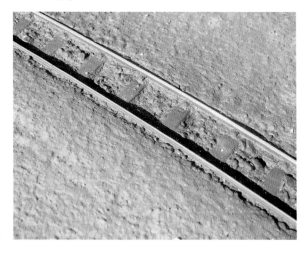

*Where track is inset in large areas of concrete roads and hard standing, it is worthwhile making the clearance around the rails a bit more generous than it would be in the prototype. Again, this promotes smooth running.*

# ELECTRIFICATION

Current is taken from mains electricity and is 'rectified' from AC to DC. It is then usually transformed down to 12 or 18V, and then two wires are attached to the track, one to each rail. Usually this current is picked up by means of metal wheels and thus drives the motor. As the rails have to be insulated from each other at all times, bare metal wheels on metal axles cannot be used.

Some form of speed control is called for and this often takes the form of a sliding resistor (rheostat) that absorbs current progressively. Because the speed is determined by the voltage reaching the motor, slow running is achieved by low voltages. These can be a bit erratic and sticky. So a refinement is electronic control whereby full voltage is applied at all times but it is being switched on and off in milliseconds. The proportion of time spent between 'on' and 'off' determines the speed. This gives a smoother control and is easier to fine-tune. An electric motor emits radio waves when it is running and this can interfere with television or radio reception locally, so it is fitted with suppressors to combat this.

In practice, the mains supply safely delivered to the workshop where it is fed into the transformer/controller. Two wires take the low current out to the track and run the trains. But if you want to run them from somewhere more convenient, a solution would be to have only the transformer in the workshop – taking low voltage to a controller situated closer to where you want it. Perhaps it could be located in a watertight box with a hinge-up lid. Plastic storage boxes from a hardware store are useful for this. Alternatively, the transformer/controller could be located indoors, with the controller itself being operated by a small portable radio-controlled transmitter.

Proprietary track systems often have small connector studs with screw tops. Wires are wound around the posts and the little nuts tightened up. But it is more convenient to solder the wires to the outside of the rails. A chunky electric iron will do the job but many people prefer to use a small gas burner. The jet is so fine that the rail can be heated without melting the plastic sleepers. As ever with soldering, cleanliness is the order of the day. It is easier to solder to brand-new track but, if it is old, then the little areas in question need to be cleaned thoroughly before tinning (applying a thin coat of solder).

Rail ends are joined by fishplates. These are tight enough to conduct current, particularly if given a whiff of WD-40, but the contact isn't absolutely reliable over time. So it is a good plan to solder small bridge wires across the joints. But it must be done using a small loop of flexible wire so that the rails can still move with expansion and contraction. When I was involved with two-rail, I preferred to use the copper braid sold for slot-car pickups. For some track systems it is possible to buy locking clamps, but they are regarded as expensive and obtrusive in some quarters. If the layout is divided into sections then insulating fishplates are used. These hold the rails in alignment but prevent any current being passed.

If you stop and think about it, where a point occurs, the crossing of the rails is a source of short-circuiting. There are two ways of getting round this. The easy way is to make the actual crossing point out of plastic and to pre-wire the point in such a way that the current flow only goes to one arm of the point. This is what most manufacturers will do. It has the added advantage that the arm of the point not in use is receiving no current. In other words, the point is self-isolating. The drawback is that the tiny bit of plastic ('dead frog') in use can mean that a short dead section can make for jerky running, but this shouldn't be too much of a problem. A more refined solution – particularly if you are planning to work to very fine tolerances – is the all-metal crossing ('live frog'). But this means that the lever operating the point also has to operate a changeover switch for the current.

Fortunately, many manufacturers supply clear guidance notes with their particular track systems and this is one occasion when it really is better to read the instructions first.

Unless you have acquired some old models, if you are coming new to the hobby it is unlikely that you will want to adopt three-rail electrification or stud contact. There are still stocks of third rail pattern chairs to be had, and members of your scale association will probably be able to provide you with information about this.

*A typical jumper lead to ensure continuity of the juice across a rail joint. The nifty little gas soldering iron did the job.*

Putting some brown colour in this final mix helps the overall effect in the garden. I use children's powder paint for the purpose. It goes against the grain to artificially paint any sort of concrete to look like nature, but we could temporarily paint or stain track areas to make them look more acceptable when brand new. Dark brown creosote substitute will give a natural-looking effect for a while but should not be repeated too often on plastic-based track.

This chapter has been a somewhat dry litany of instructions, but there is no way round it as we must get most of the basics right. As with all things, this is not as daunting as it sounds. Do the job slowly and it is finished quickly. Rush it, and it takes forever. There is much satisfaction to be had in the actual process of building a railway, out in the open air. There are times when I have been sitting in drizzle, a raindrop on the end of my nose, pinning track down. Neighbours shake their heads and the family gives me sad indulgent smiles. I am muttering that I am not enjoying myself. Only you and I know that I really am.

All of the above is a counsel of perfection. Some folk are naturally gifted at doing things perfectly and with infinite patience: not I. You may not be either. Don't panic. There is a degree of overkill in all this. Give it your best shot. If things are not perfect, you will still have a working railway.

## TRACK DESIGN

Having considered the mechanics of the track itself, perhaps we should finish off this chapter with a few thoughts about track layouts. The main requirement that the engine can run round its train. It also needs to be fed and watered, so a water tank and a coal stage are required. These may be located on the siding that leads to a small engine shed. Typically we might expect at least one siding for freight traffic, and this could well have a small goods shed to serve it. Everything else is just a refinement of this basic arrangement. In an end-to-end layout, one station would tend to be the major centre for running the railway whereas the layout at the other end will be more modest.

If you are anticipating lots of visitors to run on your line then it makes sense to install extra sidings and possibly a passing loop somewhere in the middle of your long single track. You might even consider installing a branch line so that someone else

*Track on portable layouts can come in many guises. (Photo: Ron Brown)*

*Smooth, raised track at its best. The footbridge is rather magnificent, isn't it? (Photo: Geoff Culver)*

can run another train at the same time. Tank engines are designed to run backwards or forwards equally well. So turntables are only needed if you anticipate using tender locomotives. Even so, they are not essential on narrow gauge railways. But, whatever the aesthetic qualities of your proposed layout, make sure you can reach your trains at all times!

# CHAPTER 5

# Railway Structures and Details

This is the chapter where I talk about all sorts of railway things: tunnels, bridges and the like. I will also consider the small details that add character and interest. Such features can add so much to a garden railway but can give unexpected grief as well. So a little bit of thinking beforehand comes in useful. It is a good rule of thumb to build bridges and tunnels in such a way that it looks as though they had to be built to get the railway through an obstacle, rather than having been put there for the sake of it.

## TUNNELS

There are quite a few mistakes to be made when building tunnels, but all are avoidable. Building them too small to accommodate large engines that you might own one day is a very good example. Forget about correct scale clearances (particularly on curves) and give yourself some space. *Don't* make a tunnel so long that it can't be reached comfortably from one end or the other. If you must have a long tunnel, put in access hatches somewhere.

*A tunnel can be so much more than just a hole in the ground – try to capture the feel of the damp, dark depths.*

Keep the track in a tunnel as simple as possible and lay it well. Concrete the floor rather than using loose ballast, as trains will derail in tunnels given the slightest provocation. Steam engines are rather partial to running out of steam in there too. So easy access is a must.

I have a personal preference for the inside of a tunnel to be cast to the correct profile if possible, rather than just being an obvious pile of stones inside the tunnel mouth. It looks so much better and if a train should derail, it will come to less harm against a smooth surface.

When the tunnel is complete and ready for use we can add an extra refinement: stick an aerosol of matt black paint into the tunnel and squirt liberally. It adds a realistic darkness to the interior. I once had the brainwave of coating the inside of a tunnel with soot. I put some wick material into a small tin cup and added white spirit. The effect was indeed excellent and as my arm was already filthy, I decided to add extra soot for good measure. Unfortunately, the cup fell over, spreading burning spirit over the track. The funnel effect of the tunnel turned this into a raging inferno that destroyed the track. The mess was so total that the entire area had to be demolished and started again from scratch. *Do not try this at home!*

To cast the horseshoe shape of a single-track tunnel, or the fatter shape needed for a double track, I cut end-profile boards from plywood, run some longitudinal strips into notches in these profiles and then cover with thin sheet metal of some sort. Some end-retaining boards fit outside the profiles. I paint old oil over the mould and then concrete is poured and left to set really hard. The cunning trick then is to remove the retaining boards, exposing those profile pieces. Screw a couple of substantial hooks into these and then pull them outwards. The longitudinal strips will fall down and the liner can be folded inwards at the base to make it smaller and then extracted. The liner, if neat, can even be left in place. Although this takes longer it is worth the effort.

Tunnel mouths come in all sorts of guises. They serve to hold back loose material from falling on to the track as it emerges into the light. Often built of local materials (especially brick in clay areas), they can sometimes be particularly ornate and castellated to blend in with local architecture – or the whim of a local landowner when the railway was built.

Although models of tunnel mouths can be bought as plastic kits or adapted from something else (toy plastic-moulded castles are great fun), I

*This diagrammatic model shows the method of making a profiled mould for a cast tunnel that can be collapsed afterwards.*

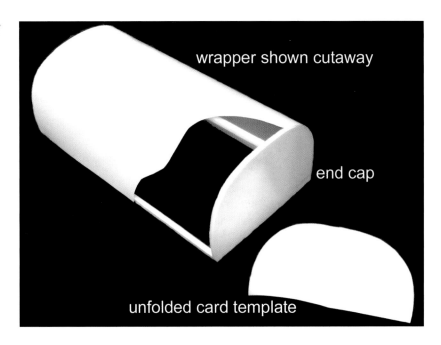

*Even humble industrial tunnels can have a realism about them – especially if invaded by some dwarf ivy.*

think they just cry out to be cast in concrete using simple home-made moulds.

## BRIDGES

Bridges are fun to build. They come in all sorts of shapes and sizes. They can be delicate 'furniture' for the railway or functional overkill. I once lavished considerable care on building a bridge with scale plastic girders that hung down from the deck. Sadly, I hadn't even had time to photograph it before my dog merrily charged through the gap underneath!

There is a school of thought that bridges should be regarded as substantial means of crossing gaps, decorated by a layer of fine detail if possible, rather than as cutting-edge economy of materials. Apart from anything else, cats will treat your bridges as their personal right of way. One bridge in my distant past was a Brunel-type, timber trestle bridge 10yd (9m) long and 4ft (1.2m) high. The deck and uprights were made of very substantial timber set in concrete. All the delicate fans were merely pinned on. It wasn't perfect in appearance but it was strong and tough. If a bridge has the appearance of having plate girder sides, a track deck of 4 × 2in (10 × 5cm) can be concealed behind the decorative sides.

Cast concrete bridges and viaducts are as strong as it gets. Wet concrete is heavy stuff and needs keeping in firm control. Although it seems such a nuisance to take the time needed to prepare strong moulds, you will regret trying to get away with using flimsy plywood and nails the first time one

*A substantial concrete viaduct by Phil Beckey. (Photo: Phil Beckey)*

*Much more rugged is this concrete viaduct by Dave Lomas. (Photo: Michael O'Hara)*

bursts open and you find yourself ankle deep in wet concrete. A strong mould, liberally oiled inside, can be used repeatedly. Thus a long viaduct can be built up from repeats of a single bridge casting devised to mate up neatly with its neighbour. It is also worthwhile marking out the sides of a mould in the form of a stone pattern and then, with a small, sharp chisel, carving the 'stones' as recesses. This is another of those jobs that is nowhere near as difficult as it sounds.

To obtain a more natural, lived-in look I would recommend making one-piece smooth-faced moulds and then removing the facing pieces when the mix is basically set but still green enough to be carved. They can be made to any size but it is worth practising with small jobs first. There are, however, many examples of moulds where the raised individual stones have been carved in reverse first. Another alternative to getting a stone finish on a smooth surface is to cast thin sheets of concrete – perhaps ¼in (6mm) thick. When it is set hard, break it up randomly into small pieces with a hammer. These can then be stuck on with waterproof white glue. When set, paint the whole thing over with white glue. It is tedious rather than skilled work but the effect can be excellent. It is also a way of upgrading an existing undetailed structure.

Slender cast structures need a good technique if they are to give us the strength we are looking for, so it is essential that the materials are really well mixed. I have found that a mix of one part cement: three parts of sharp sand and one part small gravel has given me the best delicacy/strength ratio which is durable over many years, coupled with giving a reasonable finish against a mould. I do not use builders' sand. It is a bit of a trade-off and you can read of many alternative mixes elsewhere. *Never* use beach sand for any purposes other than making sandcastles on the beach. If the structure is more bulky then the substitution of a coarser aggregate is recommended. If you plan to do a lot of concrete

*Don't feel you have to copy what you see in model railway magazines. Always keep an eye out for interesting prototype situations, like this one near Neath.*

work then a small electric cement mixer is not the luxury it sounds and will save you a great deal of hard labour over the years. It also mixes much better than you are likely to by hand. I suggest an electric one on the grounds that there are no problems with fuel or starting but, above all, the noise is much kinder to neighbours.

The received wisdom is that the usual mistake with pouring concrete is to have it too wet. What looks quite stiff on the mixing spot (or in the cement mixer), somehow becomes much wetter when it is poured and you are smoothing it down. But to cast fine detail, a wetter mix seeks out those little recesses better. Pour or trowel the mixture in gently to avoid trapping air. I like to pour a little mix into the bottom of the mould and then work it up the sides with a palette knife and a paintbrush. Add more mix in the centre and work outwards. As the depth builds up, gently tamp down the surface with a something broad and flat, such as the square end of a piece of timber. Don't stir it rapidly. Just build up the level to the top in this way then skim across the surface for neatness. If you should have need for an absolutely flat top and you are worried about your abilities with a trowel, then wrap a piece of flat wood or old kitchen worktop in clingfilm and use it as a weight to work over the surface.

Intricate, recessed detail in bridges can also make use of the 'lost core' technique, whereby shaped pieces of polystyrene foam are very lightly pinned to the inside of the mould. When the face of

the mould is struck, the foam remains in place. After a few days the concrete is hard enough to allow us to dig out chunks of foam and then dissolve away the remainder with cellulose thinners.

Most of everything above holds good if you want to cast concrete platforms. It would make sense to cast them twice as deep as they should be and then to bury half of that depth in the ground. Within a week it looks like something that will remain untroubled until the end of time. However, if you try to skimp things, then cracks will start appearing after a few years. I know only too well that there is a natural tendency to want to push on and get things done, but taking time to do things right in the first place is by far the best strategy.

## ALTERNATIVE BRIDGE MATERIALS

There are all sorts of other ways to build bridges. One is to use a piece of $4 \times 2$in ($10 \times 5$cm) sawn, pressure-treated timber. This is our durable trackbed. Then we glue and pin stripwood along the side to make it look like the edge of a girder, so the track seems to be running along the top of a girder bridge. If your bridge is located so that it is impossible to see it from behind, you might, quite sensibly, be tempted not to bother with the back. Look for suitable plastic mouldings that can be pinned to the edge of the board to suggest girder construction – bakers' trays, beer crates and the like are good for this.

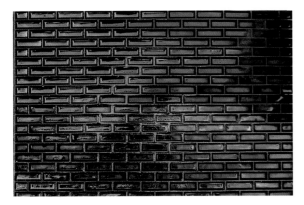

*A rubber car mat, suitably oiled up and mounted on a backing board, makes a useful mould for stone-block walls – suitable for bridge supports and retaining walls. . . .*

Perhaps I should mention metal bridges. If you have access to a large quantity of strip metal, for some reason or another, it is downright criminal not to make use of it. For some specific applications you might consider buying strip from a stockist and assembling it with pop rivets or welding. It may be that you would like to make a realistic model of a specific sort of bridge, rather than have something vaguely generic. In that case it becomes like any other form of scale model-making. You need to buy the correct materials in the first place and not mind the cost. If you have a natural inclination for such

*. . . and here is what it looks like when cast. The old steelworks loco has seen better days.*

*A slightly modified version of this will eventually support a bridge. It makes good sense to put a few bits of wood and track in place, as I have done here, to help visualize what the end result will look like.*

*A splendidly elegant bowstring bridge on Alan Millichamp's line. It is made of welded rod.*

*Rough-sawn softwood strip is the material used for this trestle bridge. It has been out of doors for many years and remains in good heart due to an annual spray with cheap fence preservative.*

things, you can build some magnificent structures by welding. Take a look at a Marty Cozad example in Chapter 16.

Timber trestle bridges are particularly satisfying to build. But instead of buying large quantities of ready-cut stripwood at enormous expense, use the money to buy a tablesaw that has at least an 8in (20cm) diameter blade. Then you can rip up your own strips out of cheap planks and be much more versatile. I like to use softwood because it absorbs preservative better and accepts pins more easily. Incidentally, when assembling timber strip bridges, you may find it difficult to knock the pins in using a pin hammer. It is better to resort to squeezing them into place with a large pair of pliers. You might think that just pinning thin strips, without the use of glue, would make for a fairly weak structure. But if you follow prototype design, there are so many pins that, in the end, the whole thing has a surprising integral strength. Finally, if you plan to have a lot of intricate bridgework, buy a cheap electric spraygun. It makes repainting them with preservative a matter of minutes instead of hours (or days!).

One group of bridges that we may well encounter are those that hinge upwards to allow us access. They can vary from the simple and functional to fine-scale models of prototype structures. In the cause of simplicity and reliability, I have favoured the former. There are just so many alternative ways of achieving this goal that I will refrain from laying down any rules and leave it to your ingenuity. But there is one useful dodge that applies to many of

*Timber trestle bridges can achieve huge proportions – especially in US garden railways. The designs tend to follow this more modest example.*

them. Build the bridge, complete with its locating devices, and then lay the track across it in one continuous piece. Fix it down really well. Install any locking and locating devices. Only then cut the rails. This will contribute to smooth running across the bridge.

## TURNTABLES

It is possible to buy ready-made turntables if you like a simple life, but there are all sorts of ways of building them. A defunct alloy record turntable deck and its bearing will provide 90 per cent of a

*Brian Spring's neat lift-up bridge gives access to an inner area.*

*A functional but simple home-made turntable gives access to several steam-up sidings.*

railway turntable straight away. If there is an old car wheel bearing lurking away at the back of the garage then that is splendidly durable. For a large turntable it might be worth insetting a lorry wheel into the ground, to form a circular track for roller wheels at the ends of the deck to run round on. Working on the principle that simple is best, a little brass barrel bolt fitted at each end of the deck can be slid outwards into short lengths of tubing to locate the rail ends accurately. I did once try using ball catches for click location but found them trickier to adjust to reliable operation. There are also plenty of different nylon door catches, intended for kitchen cupboards, that you can experiment with.

All of this technology suits the meatiness of live steam engines. With two-rail electrification however, we have the problem of getting the juice to the deck, and making sure it reverses polarity when

the track has changed ends. To make the track on the turntable permanently live, the best method is to make some form of slip rings. Around the central bearing there are two concentric brass rings fitted to the ground. Brushes from slot-racing model cars rub along these and so pick up the current. But there is still a possibility of conflicting current when the engine moves off the turntable on to the fixed track. To avoid this would call for either permanent concentration or some form of electronic interlocking. Alternatively, we could substitute jack plugs around the outside of the turntable, arranged so that they would slide into a fixed jack socket at either end of the deck. If the current in use was too high for safety then there is a variety of alternative small plugs and sockets available that can be adapted to form locks as well. For most practical purposes we can enjoy the simplicity of rotating the turntable by hand. As well as the commercially available examples, which are powered, it is fairly easy to make a suitably low-geared mechanism from the scrap box, but be careful as it can be pretty noisy. One method is to clip a small electric screwdriver to the underside of the deck and make a tool to go in the socket that holds a small foam rubber wheel. This will rotate against the base of the turntable well – typically concrete – and do the business for you. You will need to alter the screwdriver to incorporate an external on/off switch instead of the inconvenient press-to-hold one already fitted.

*A more detailed working turntable on a continental G-scale layout. (Photo: courtesy* Die Gartenbahn)

*A built-in steam-raising area is a useful structure – particularly for spirit-fired engines.*

For unusual situations, particularly in limited areas, there are more straightforward alternatives to a turntable for merely switching tracks. A sector plate is a short piece of track, pivoted at one end so that the other can swing around a part of a circle. This occupies less space than points. A traverser is a short length of track that can roll sideways on its own rails, typically found in locomotive works.

Both of these are simple and cheap to make, if you really are very tight for engine shunting space in a tight corner. Perhaps in this category too we could mention cable haulage for shunting. Powered capstans drag vehicles in and out of small spaces. It is rather a quaint option but fun to try and easily modelled. In the garden gauges we have absolutely perfect non-slip capstans, ready to be motorized, available in the form of the little rubber stubbers that go on the ends of walking sticks. Incidentally, they also make useful small bollards on a model quayside.

*Whilst we are on the subject of steaming up, how about this for natty simplicity?*

# SIGNALS

Signals on garden railways mean different things to different people. At one end of the spectrum are those for whom proper signalling is one of the most significant factors of running any sort of railway. At the other, we will encounter those for whom signals are an unnecessary evil. In between are those who like to see them as pieces of jewellery that highlight the overall picture. But whatever the perception, the practical considerations remain the same.

Wooden signal posts will tend to rot despite preservatives being applied during construction.

*Signal kits are widely available and need no elaboration. But narrow gauge practice offers the chance to model some very ethnic prototypes.*

Because signals are delicate and intricate structures that are time consuming to overhaul, if you plan to have a lot of them, it might be a good idea to prepare a batch beforehand and ask your timber yard to pressure-treat them for you. It is better to paint them with a 'soak-in' coat, referred to as a 'garden colours' finish than apply something that has a protective skin like conventional paint. This is much easier to touch up in subsequent years.

Signal posts made of brass tube are very durable and the bits of detail can be soldered or bolted on. Metal details can be glued to wooden posts but the movement of natural wood tends to break many bonded joints with inert materials over time. I have cast signal posts in fibreglass resin but they are, as might be expected, prone to snap. Glass-filled nylon would be better. The mechanics of operating signals are quite delicate but many examples of correctly operated systems have appeared. There is a particular pleasure in making the signal wires return cranks and operating levers. I have to admit that it has escaped me thus far but it certainly works for some.

Signals operated by solenoids are common. This is indoor model railway technology in a waterproof box. Most of what is available is of non-British prototypes but it is fairly straightforward to get a British appearance by changing or modifying the arms and tweaking a few details. Purists may be unhappy about the incorrect detail, but years of trouble-free operation should keep the smile on your face. Signals can, like points, also be operated by a commercial compressed air system.

Coloured light signals are a more modern alternative and are, of course, easier to control. In my early days, home-made ones were produced by buying glass tubing and bending it over a Bunsen burner. A concealed light bulb would shine up from the bottom and the light would be bent round by internal reflection under the paint finish, to shine out at the top of the post. Strips of coloured celluloid would be pulled across the gap between bulb and tube to change colour. Nowadays, with LEDs (light emitting diodes) that comfortably fit into scale size housings, life is much easier. If you don't want to buy ready-made colour signal lights then set up a production line for making batches of them in various sections of brass tubing and section.

## EXAMPLES OF INTERESTING DETAILS

*A dockside steam crane can be an intricate model in its own right. If you enjoy scratchbuilding, this is real fun.*

*The top of this water tank was made by gluing 35mm colour-slide holders to a wood block. It sits on a timber framework made by Dave Pinniger.*

*Even the style of a simple station name board can help set the tone of a garden railway.*

*You can't get much simpler than a used can and pieces of old sleepers!*

## SMALLER DETAILS

These come in a huge range of shapes and sizes. Much is inexpensive and available commercially, but there are plenty of home-made alternatives. Many simple things can be made from nails and wire. Old flexible track that is too far-gone for reliable use can sometimes be turned on edge, with the rail side away from view. We can also juggle scales. If the railway is to one of the garden gauges, then old 00-gauge track can make model garden fencing. Even old budgie cages or rabbit wire can be put to good use. By snipping away in the right places,

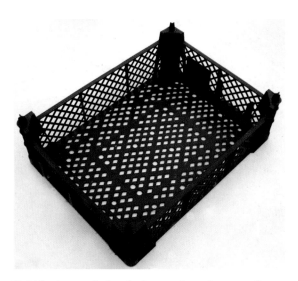

*'Soft' fencing can be bought from garden railway suppliers, but it can also be adapted from many other sources. You can buy woven natural edging or weave it yourself from basket-weave materials. Look out for disposable plastic fruit trays – preferably in a dark colour because paint does not like to stick to the soapy plastic. I am particularly fond of plastic drainer mats that can be cut into strips to form ornate ironwork.*

quite a bit of strong fencing of uprights and fence rails can be cut out. They may well rust with time but still give good service. Moreover, they can be bent to different shapes and angles.

Realistic buffer stops can be bought or easily made. On narrow gauge railways they can be as simple as a few old wooden sleepers pinned together. My only pertinent observation is that if you have a track that ends in a drop of several feet to a concrete path, then don't mess about: either

concrete a nice bit of stone in place or fix a sturdy piece of wood to the end of the baseboard.

Telegraph poles, especially if correctly strung with wire, look splendid. They can really add to the railway atmosphere. Unfortunately, they have a great capacity for spoiling your day as they are delicate and easily ruined by a single starling or the careless brush of a sleeve. There is a sort of convention that accepts the idea of the posts being there but left unstrung. If so, for the sake of a long life for both yourself and the posts, I wouldn't bother with lots of little bits of wood. I would use ready-made plastic ones. To kill the plastic look, drag some coarse sandpaper along the lengths of the post to increase the grain and get rid of the shine. For a really well-weathered look, rub in a mix of light grey and olive-green acrylic bathroom paint with a cloth.

If you have your heart set on strung poles, very fine copper wire is usually best otherwise things can look crude and clumsy. A good source of this might be the windings off an old mains-voltage electric motor or a transformer. Kinked wires do not look good so pull them out by holding one end in a vice and then tugging with a pair of pliers from a distance. It is important that the beginning of the 'run' of wires doesn't start from an unsupported post otherwise it will lean inwards under tension. The end posts need to be diagonally stayed down to the ground with a tougher wire, maybe even including a tension spring.

An alternative is to use thin fishing-line. Nylon monofilament has a nice degree of springiness in it, which is useful. You will soon discover that a simple knot immediately slides undone. This is fine when you twist the line around intermediate insulators but not much use at the ends. Ask a fisherman about his little knot to overcome this. Whilst you are talking to him, get him to show you a tiny snaplink at the same time. It is quite a useful gadget. The main alternative to monofilament is something like a fine-braided Terylene. This is not stretchy but is tough and easier to tie. It might be worth incorporating a small tension spring at the end of a run of line to keep things looking neat and tidy. It also has the advantage that it can be wiped over with some wood stain to colour it. From everything I have said, you will gather that it makes sense to put a run of strung telegraph posts behind the running line

*There is more to water on a railway than just fishponds. The dock area of this 2½in garden railway adds another dimension. An option for us weathering enthusiasts is to add a dash of green and brown poster paint to the water occasionally. (Photo: Paul Cooper)*

rather than in front. Don't let me put you off erecting some by my gloomy warnings. When done properly it really does look good.

Whatever scale you work in, there will be an endless variety of accessories and small scenic details to be purchased over the counter. A station platform is brought to life with bits of luggage, milk churns, little trolleys and so on. I am sure that you will enjoy browsing through catalogues and buying these – I certainly do. But there are DIY alternatives. Carving and sanding a suitcase from a piece of balsa wood is a simple thing to start with. It costs virtually nothing and the sense of satisfaction at having done it is considerable. For items you might want a lot of, consider mass production. If, for example, I wanted fifty milk churns, I would make a master in aluminium. I have a lathe but if I did not, I would turn it up by holding it in the chuck of an electric drill (held in a horizontal stand) and worry it into shape with files. I would then make a mould in hot re-meltable rubber. From this I could take many resin castings. More than one cottage industry has started this way.

Try not to become so absorbed in the scale of what you model that you are blind to other things that can be adapted. A battered Dinky toy lorry trailer can make a platform trolley in the garden gauges. A big pig in one scale can be a small one in another.

You will develop an obsession about visiting toy and souvenir shops looking for suitable accessories of the right scale. You will learn to curse the fact that many otherwise suitable cars and lorries are to 1:16th, 1:18th or 1:25th scale, none of which are quite right for common garden railway scales. The Gauge-1-ers can smile smugly at the ranges of

1:32nd scale model soldiers (a crawling soldier converts to a superb rock climber), farm sets and slot-racing equipment that is readily available. The rest of us smile through gritted teeth and continue to seek unlikely sources of supply, such as model boat fittings.

## THE LITTLE PEOPLE

Model human figures, like the prototypes, can have their problems. Beauty is in the eye of the modeller. I have good friends who get much pleasure from their plastic models of Snow White and her entourage, Grommit, Darth Vader and the Sheriff of Nottingham on their layouts. There are also – how may I put this delicately? – examples of model ladies who are not even wearing their vests and must be getting quite chilly. If such things figure in your ambitions then enjoy them wholeheartedly. However, if you are looking for realism, there are one or two useful hints to consider. Even the most garish plastic figure can be enhanced by a muted paint job, as is described in Chapter 9. I could never get on with articulated toy figures. They seemed to need so much work to disguise their appearance that it was quicker to make them from new. But you may see things differently.

You can, of course, invent some characters to inhabit your railway. I have quite a few and many more who exist only as sketches for now, but who will become three-dimensional realities one day. Modelling compound such as Fimo, over a wire armature, can be used. Even child's modelling clay will make a durable model, which will go quite hard over time. I am no expert in this department but

*The little people: getting a natural grouping makes a difference. If at all possible, try to dispense with moulded plastic bases and replace them with a pin or similar.*

the secret seems to be not to try to model the complete character in one lump. Instead, make the basic body and maybe the legs. Add the head. Then use thin-rolled modelling compound to 'dress' the figure. If you are a natural wood-carver then exploit your talent.

Because the garden gauges can be quite chunky, there is room for a bit of ingenuity. For example, a workman can be made to shovel ballast. He will be fitted to a deep base that contains a geared electric motor. This drives a rod, through a lever, to move the arms appropriately. This is most practically achieved by making a base container for the motor, mechanism and battery, with the figure fitted on top. He can then 'plug in' to a location on the railway. It makes for an interesting modelling project and brings pleasure to others. One example that springs to mind was a prize-winning model of a wagon being pushed along by a properly walking man.

But there are things we can do at a simpler level. If a figure has a cast base on it, saw and file it away, then drill up one leg and insert a length of stiff wire (I particularly like the redundant tails off small pop rivets). The figures can then be plugged into holes drilled into platforms, streets and so on. One aesthetic point

that some consider important, is to avoid little people that are frozen in action poses. Some modellers don't mind but to others it is anathema. A similar argument relates to loco crew. Folk can get quite bothered by a locomotive that is not being driven by actual figures (the *Marie Celeste* effect). Others couldn't care less or say *they* are the crew. So go with what you want. There can be no doubt that the presentation and placement of figures can add to the general appearance of a railway; however, if your layout is a functional track upon which to run long trains then you can happily ignore them altogether.

As I like to install details and figures that will add to realism rather than detract from it, I prefer not to have something that is the wrong scale or very plastic looking. Some owners of garden railways need to see a great many little people, animals and similar details. Others prefer a sort of clean sparseness, and yet others just don't care. You will find your own natural level with this. With the smaller fittings in particular, your collection will seem to grow of its own accord. You can plan and scheme all you want, but then you see an old-fashioned mangle sitting on top of a pencil sharpener. Resistance is useless and the next thing you know . . . .

*Let's round this chapter off with something that doesn't know if it is a railway structure, a big detail or a building. When the basic railway is up and running, there is no reason why you shouldn't really enjoy yourself with an ambitious model in its own right. For example, here's a beam engine house under construction, something you could really get your teeth into. Down in the bottom right I put in a lorry windscreen wiper motor to provide the drive powered by a small 12V gel battery.*

# CHAPTER 6

# Locomotives

Now we get on to one of the juiciest bits. I think that, truth be told, most of us regard the engines we run as being at the very heart of the hobby, and some of us have far too many for our needs. We try to think up reasons for always wanting more: knowing full well that we are kidding no one. To the newcomer, this may seem academic. As he browses

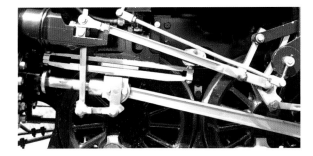

through catalogues we hear the despairing cry, '*How much?*' There is no getting away from the fact that model locomotives in larger scales can seem expensive to eyes accustomed to the modest demands of their smaller brothers indoors.

But things are not as bad as they seem. A successful garden railway can work with just one engine. If you want many more, there are plenty of devious routes to achieve this. You could, for example, buy a small battery-powered toy car for peanuts, pull off the wheels and replace them with a set of railway wheels. All that remains to be done is to throw the body away and you have a little working chassis. It is the work of an hour to make a small freelance diesel loco body in card, balsa or plastic. You are in business. Your little loco trundles along the track and all is well with the world. It may not win any engineering prizes but it is your first-born and will remain forever locked in your affection. This principle will later extend to making more ambitious bodies and also to adapting cheap toy trains you may encounter.

The next step is to buy rudimentary chassis kits and start to think about more realistic bodies to go on top. Diesel-outline locomotives are often little more than a couple of interestingly shaped boxes. A sheet of plastic card or cardboard – even very thin ply – will provide most of the locomotive

*The Aster Flying Scotsman in gauge 1. A superb live steam model that represents a considerable outlay all wrapped up in one model, but worth saving up for as it can be the focal point of an entire garden railway. (Photo: courtesy Aster UK)*

*An ex LMS 4-4-0 in 0 gauge. This is the sort of conventional two-rail model that is usually built from an etched kit, and represents the standard sort of workhorse of a garden railway. (Photo: Phil Beckley)*

*But more traditional methods of building are available to us. The body of this 0-gauge tank engine is built mostly of card and runs on an old Lima chassis.*

outline. Ingenuity and a rummage through the scrap box will do the rest. A steam loco will additionally call for several short tubes. An entire workshop can fit into a shoebox and costs are negligible. It mirrors a full-size world of tiny backwoods railways being held together with string, prayers and no money. You can model this and find it utterly delightful.

## BARGAINS

Going to shows and meetings may expose you to bargain bins of odds and ends. An old plastic diesel loco body with a crack in it can be fixed. It may cost a small amount or even nothing at all. On the whole, garden railway enthusiasts are a kind bunch who remember their early struggles and are happy to help out a beginner. You in turn will adopt a similar approach later on as you get established and comfortable. On the other hand, always trying to go for the cheapest option can get you into trouble. If someone offers an old steam engine on the Internet at a cheap price, it may be a genuine bargain or it may be unusable for some reason, and need more skill than you have right now to fix. There have been well-meaning small outfits that built steam engines for sale, without really understanding what was needed. In some cases they were so badly designed that it was impossible for them to actually work and could only be fixed with a lot of skilled rebuilding. Even worse were models that were built badly and with such unsuitable material that by the time everything had been rectified, there was literally *nothing* left of the original model. I know it sounds like very obvious advice but don't let your common sense take a sudden holiday just because you see a low price tag.

*Simple ready-to-run plastic: an LGB diesel shunter is unpretentious but will be trouble-free for many years.*

*A further refinement comes in the form of this simple pantograph loco from LGB. It can collect power from the rails or the overhead wiring. (Photo: courtesy* Die Gartenbahn)

## READY-TO-RUN PLASTIC

Narrow gauge in the garden gauges is extensively served by ready-to-run electric trains that pick up current from the track. The bodies will mostly be in tough plastic with some metal fittings. The prototypes are modelled on European or US practice and the range is enormous. There are tiny diesel shunters, huge steam-outline locomotives that have more wheels than seems decent, and all steps between. Browsing through catalogues is a most enjoyable occupation and you will be following an honourable tradition when you indulge in it. They induce immediate feelings of wanton lust and need little further comment from me. Being large-scale

*More power now: a US outline bogie diesel is designed for some serious train hauling. Such things can often come with sophisticated sound systems and hi-tech digital command and control (DCC), but at heart it is still a rugged two-rail locomotive with a tough plastic body.*

locomotives, there is often enough space to fit battery packs inside if you are not into two-rail. A useful source of suitable rechargeable batteries, over and above the common ones, are those sold specifically for model aircraft. G scalers in particular often make good use of these. It is also possible to fit batteries in 0-gauge locomotives that are fitted with 12V motors designed for two-rail pickup. Ingenious folk can also squeeze radio control into a tender or a van next to the loco.

## LOCOMOTIVE KITS

Kits come in all shapes and sizes. There are simple things that can be had for loose change, and there are boxes full of exquisite etched-brass components that call for considerable skill to assemble and paint. My feeling is that it is better to build a simple kit and enjoy running it, rather than spend a lot of money on something that ends up looking like it has had a nasty accident and doesn't work. However, if you have experience of kits in indoor scales, then by all means bring it to the table and make use of it.

0-gauge fine-scale standard gauge seems to be mostly centred on white-metal and etched-brass kits in the UK. They range from things that are almost as simple to assemble as a plastic kit right

*A further example of a kit made from plastic card pieces. But this time it is sitting on a home-made 32mm gauge chassis.*

up to being convenient packs of resources for what is virtually skilled scratchbuilding. However, beware of reviews in magazines by well-meaning experts who have a somewhat optimistic view of the word 'simple'. If you are coming into the hobby without background experience, then take yourself along to exhibitions and actually talk to people. This seems to be a better source of practical advice at grass roots level. Similar technology can also be had in gauge 1.

Let us briefly look at building locos this way. The easiest kits are where the chassis virtually bolts together and the body is made up of white-metal castings that can be glued together. The instructions will be comprehensive and there may be a diagram as well. You may also want to do some research on a model: to find photographs and drawings. This is particularly true if you have an interest in accurate modelling of a specific prototype and all its variations. As with all kits, it is essential to work on a flat surface. It also makes a big difference if you are sitting comfortably and the area is well lit. A good etched-brass kit will have fold lines etched in and it is easy to press over a tab at a right angle by catching part of the job in the jaws of a vice and then pushing sideways with a steel ruler. But those serrated jaws will mark the

*A plastic-card kit for a British outline, tank engine body designed to fit an LGB chassis.*

*Assembling the final components of a US etched-brass kit. This example featured many lost wax brass castings and was a comparatively easy example to build. Some kits call for a very high level of skill.*

*Most models will withstand getting wet. This diesel loco is mostly built in mild steel and has been in use for many years in all weathers.*

brass. So make up a couple of liners out of thin bent metal or even just thin cardboard.

Soldering (including low-temperature solder) is covered elsewhere. Always remember to clean a soldered joint afterwards, using warm soapy water and a toothbrush. My favourite alternative is to soak a job overnight in Steradent. If you are really nervous about delicate soldering then you can use superglue in conjunction with Roket powder to form fillets. But it really is worthwhile getting used to soldering.

A good kit will not expect you to roll boilers and the like out of flat sheet. I have to confess that I prefer to try to avoid this task. Where it is needed, I search out a tube of some sort, and then fake things

up around it. If you are building a tender engine, it is usually best to build the tender first. This gives you an easier introduction to the building techniques and also to the way that the manufacturer 'thinks'. There can be quite a bit of variation in the way kits are produced – and what they demand of the builder. It is certainly wise, with the loco itself, to build a smoothly rolling chassis first. When satisfied, go on to motorize it according to the instructions. A wonky chassis that runs erratically will not work any better by having a body fitted on top of it and painted. So get any tweaking done first.

Allow plenty of time to assemble your first sophisticated kit. Steadily work through the stages at a comfortable pace and don't even think about looking forward to the end product. In particular, there is a very human tendency to rush the last parts of the building and painting.

Most metal or plastic model locomotives can be run out of doors satisfactorily. The motors won't come to any harm and a spray of WD-40 takes care of most problems. Trains will pick up current from the track, even on a wet day. The problems to watch out for mostly concern anything that will rust. So connecting rods shaped from mild steel might be vulnerable. But live steamers – and the real thing – use materials like this all the time so don't worry too much. If you have a really exquisite fine-scale 0-gauge locomotive that has got soaked, just give it a few minutes with a hair-dryer afterwards. But not many people bother. The only fitting that seems to suffer in wet conditions is you, the driver.

## LIVE STEAM

### 'Gather friends, whilst we enquire into trains propelled by fire'
(*Steam in the Garden*)

I am going to allow a personal prejudice to show through here. I think that, out in the garden, it is live steam that gives the best magic of all. There are simple elemental forces at work as our small drag-ons run under a real sky, through living greenery. They are not models; they are steam engines in their own right, driven by fire.

The trade can supply a large array of live steam engines. They will mostly be user-friendly and aimed at the non-engineer. Some will have a simple outline and not too many bolt-on extras. They are well suited to running trains simply. Do not assume that the most expensive, most complex model is automatically the best for your needs. We may all lust after the dream machines but a simple engine may actually give more pleasure as far as day-to-day running is concerned.

## A STEAM RUN

Let us take a run behind that simple engine. It sits there, cold and inanimate, on the track. These days

*A simple live steam engine, built around Accucraft Ruby components. It is a workhorse model of an early mineral locomotive and is easy to run.*

*A scratchbuilt Guinness locomotive with the steam controls easily accessible. There are fresh challenges around every corner.*

it will probably be gas fired so the first step is to top up the tank using a little adapter screwed into a small butane canister. The gas tank briefly acquires a layer of frost. We make sure that any gas vapour has dispersed and then think about topping the boiler up. Distilled water is squirted into the boiler, using a large disposable syringe. In the early days you may measure the quantity out carefully but, after a while, you will get used to peeking into the filler opening and judging the right level. The cap is screwed back in. The next step is to top up the displacement lubricator with proper steam oil (*never* car oil!).

The lubricator is ingeniously simple. Before a run, it is filled with oil. At the end of the steam-up this will have turned to oily water – and there are no moving parts. Put a drop of light oil around the

*For the non-engineer, there is usually some very easy route into live steam. This Java steam tram (believed to have been converted from a steam crane) was built around an old Mamod stationary engine by a very young enthusiast on pocket money of 2/- (10p) a week.*

visible moving components such as the axle bearings, motion rods and so on. A good rule of thumb is that oil is cheaper than steam engines so, when in doubt, oil it. But do not put oil into the boiler – it degrades the efficiency of steam raising, and is very difficult to clean out properly afterwards.

Wiping down metal soon becomes an automatic process. It doesn't cost anything and that gets my vote. But now it is time to light up. The gas valve is turned on and a cigarette lighter is applied to, in this case, the top of the chimney. There will be a loud popping sound followed by a slight roar that tells us all is well. Making sure that the regulator is shut, leave the engine and walk along the track, making sure that no leaves or twigs have fallen across it and that any points are set correctly.

Whilst this is being done, the water is boiling. One of the nice things about a live steam engine is that it talks to us. It hisses and sighs and, in doing so, it tells us things. Even without a pressure gauge, we know what is happening in the boiler; we feel it coming to life. It is time to open the regulator . . .

and nothing happens. There may be a slight jerk and a spit of steam but the wheels are locked solid. Steam going into the cold cylinders has condensed and there is a hydraulic lock. So we close the regulator and maybe give our engine a slight nudge before opening it again.

This is a time for patience. Those cylinders will warm up in a short while. But for now, we may be treated to great gobs of hot oily water being spat out of the chimney in a most undignified fashion. But we feel the engine become free and eager to be off. At this stage I usually let it run a short distance and back before wiping it clean. As a precaution, I also like to give it a run around the track as a light engine first before adding a train behind it, as I might have missed something in the track inspection and don't want to deal with re-railing an entire string of wagons.

So the engine runs: a free spirit. The white steam trails out behind and the magic is there again. It is time to run a train. It is a matter of pride that we can back our engine to the coaches we will

*This gauge 1 model of Lion is an affordable introduction to Aster models. It really does look very pretty when running. (Photo: courtesy Aster UK)*

*A good general-purpose steam locomotive – built at home – for gauge 1. It is not as svelte as some designs but it has a purposeful look to it. (Photo: Geoff Culver)*

*Something more elegant: this B12 has inside cylinders. Practical live steam, with few concessions to appearance, is why the gods invented gauge 1. (Photo: Geoff Culver)*

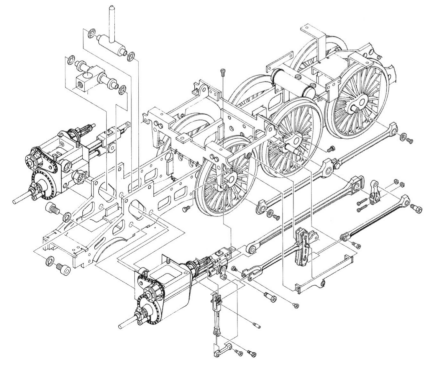

*We can de-mystify the apparently complicated nature of a steam-engine chassis by reference to a diagram. The two mainframes hold the wheels in the right place and support the cylinders. Those intricate-looking rods and levers connect things together but may be bolted on and off individually. (Drawing: courtesy Aster UK)*

*A Cardean in any scale is a work of art in its own right. This gauge 1 example looks superb in motion. You can understand why anyone is prepared to put a great deal of time into loco building when you see something like this. (Photo: Geoff Culver)*

*This Aster German Kriegslok nicely shows up the chassis pieces in real metal. (Photo: courtesy Aster UK)*

*We conclude this short group of inspirational models with a picture of a gauge 1 Gresley 2-8-2. And here we are getting pretty close to the mountain top. But it does no harm to raise our eyes and aspire to such things. (Photo: Geoff Culver)*

be pulling today simply by adjusting the regulator so that it creeps up until there is the faintest kiss of buffers. I use small hook and chain couplings, so I hook the links over with my pliers. Have a quick look round to check that all is well, and then open the regulator to just the right setting, and stand back and watch as the train slowly accelerates up to a comfortable narrow gauge speed. There is a whole panoply of tiny noises to enjoy. Metal wheels in particular drum splendidly on the track and there may be a faint tinkling of couplings and the tapping of buffers. The engine can be heard faintly chuffing away. All of these sounds vary as the train goes behind walls or over bridges. Onwards our train runs, slowing and quickening in response to curves and slight gradients. Time stands still.

When the run is over, the engine is uncoupled and, with the last dregs of steam pressure, run to a siding for disposal. The lubricator drain cock is opened and the final wisps of stream drive out the oily water. Fresh oil is added now. There is a lovely patina to be had when warm metal is polished with a slightly oily rag. This is model machinery at its best; it even smells right. Whilst the engine is cooling down, we shall leave it there, sitting quietly. This can be a rewarding hobby.

## RADIO CONTROL

Modestly priced plug-and-play technology means that radio control is a common option for operating battery-powered or live steam locomotives. There will be a hand-held transmitter that usually has two or more channels and a receiver fitted in the engine itself. To convert received signals into mechanical motion that moves levers, little gadgets called servos are needed. To vary the speed of battery-powered locos, an alternative is a speed controller circuit. If you buy the equipment separately it will all come in a set, together with instructions. But it may well come ready fitted to a commercial locomotive.

The small joysticks on the transmitter will operate controls by degrees, rather than just being 'on/off', and this is generally referred to as Proportional Radio Control. Simple operation of live steam might involve the use of just one joystick, which would operate a valve on the loco to give a degree of speed control. It usually requires the engine to be manually reversed before setting off. But there is a degree of refinement that makes use of the expansive quality of steam. When an engine is starting to pull away, it needs plenty of steam for each stroke. But when running at speed, on level track in particular, the amount of puff per stroke can be less. This is called notching-up and is an essential part of full-size live steam operation. Down in our tiny sizes we are not worried about the marginal savings of cost that this offers. But it adds to the challenge of good driving as well as giving remote control of reversing. To all intents and purposes, a simplified form of Walschearts valve gear is called for, rather than slip-eccentric gear, to obtain this more advanced facility.

All forms of radio transmissions are allocated specific frequency bands, to avoid conflicts. These are legally enforceable. Ground-based models in the UK mostly use the 40MHz band; mostly replacing the older 27Hz AM format. This can be subdivided into thirty-four separate frequencies so that different models can operate together. This is determined by whichever colour-coded crystal you have plugged into your equipment at the time. You are required to have a pennant attached to the top of your transmitter aerial which has a matching colour, so that you are visibly displaying the colour you are using. Incidentally, it is a good idea to have a plastic or foam ball impaled on the tip of your antenna to avoid stabbing someone in the face when you suddenly turn round!

The range of these transmitters is (deliberately) limited, compared to the aeromodelling band of 35Mhz, which you are not allowed to use. But all of these considerations are taken care of by the suppliers. If you buy a ready-made commercial locomotive, everything will be as it should. All you have to do is read the instructions and enjoy yourself.

The signal from an aircraft transmitter has a much longer range and is uncluttered by interference. However, our railway is surrounded by all sorts of metal things – including track, fence wire and even the metal of the engine itself. So it is possible for signals to be reflected and so return to the receiver microseconds later than the main signal.

*A transmitter tends to look rather complicated but is designed to be light to hold and easy to use.*

This is not long but can be enough to confuse it. Control can be erratic. This is widely known as the 'rusty-bolt' effect (because rusty connections can sometimes give rise to the same phenomenon). If you suffer from this problem in your own garden (it isn't inevitable), you may get to know where to stand to avoid it. But there is add-on commercial circuitry that can help combat this.

There is also quite a lot of metal in the loco itself, which may affect the signal. Sometimes it is possible to coil the aerial way out of sight but this may be difficult on a live steam model, where some areas get too hot. A large dome on the boiler, if insulated from it, can make a good aerial. But more typically a 2in (5cm) square of brass is glued to the underside of the cab roof, with some intervening insulation material such as plastic card. A particularly good aerial, which will receive the signal strongly from all directions, is a pyramid made of thin brass and hidden under a dummy coal load in a loco tender.

Radio control makes for very convenient operation. There is a permanent 'hands-on' feel to the driving and its appeal is self-evident. A variation of this theme can apply to two-rail electrification. Current is fed to the track conventionally, but a small hand-held transmitter controls the adjustment of that current. This means that you can fol-

low the trains around, uncoupling and shunting them, without continually having to return to the control panel.

To its adherents, driving by radio control gives a feeling of being there in the cab. So what does it all feel like? A transmitter seems a bit light and flimsy but the little spring-loaded levers fall under the thumb easily enough. With an engine in steam and everything ready to go, that first experimental waggle of the lever causes a nervous moment. But after a few minutes the engine will move at your command. Most transmitters have little trim tabs that adjust the action of the main levers, and you might want to fiddle with those in due course. But content yourself for now with getting the whole 'feel' of everything. There is a tangible inertia from the mass of the locomotive, which is heightened if you have the weight of a train behind it. You soon discover that gradients and curves need to be compensated for. Getting a locomotive to back gently on to a train is an art in itself. It may seem strange at first but it gradually sinks into the subconscious and you will soon be driving well without the need for premeditated thought.

You also become aware that, like the real thing, different live steam locomotives have their own characteristics. Some are docile workhorses that are easy to look after and drive. Others are more skittish and highly-strung. You may encounter a loco that goes better in one direction than the other. Yet again, there is the engine that likes to tip-toe through points a bit more slowly. It all mirrors full-size practice. Enjoy the act of learning all this, for you are becoming an engine driver.

Do remember though that radio control isn't compulsory. There are those of our number who prefer not to use it: not because of some reaction against technology but because they feel that trains should be run free, dependent upon the skill of the operator. If you are in this camp, don't let yourself be talked into radio control by those of the other persuasion. One final thought: a good live steam model should be capable of running well with manual operation. Radio control should be an extra that enables operation to be convenient, not something essential to tame an otherwise uncontrollable beast.

The gas firing mentioned earlier has replaced the dominance of methylated spirits (spirit firing) to a large degree. But, whichever is used, there are various ways of letting their flames heat the water. The simplest is the externally fired potboiler. Here, the fire is at ordinary air pressure and requires no artificial draught. It is easy to control and is more tolerant of gradients. Early locomotives used to be flaming fireballs in the slightest breeze. But a shield concealed behind side tanks, and better draughting, has improved things beyond measure. Archangel models transformed potboilers into well-engineered, high-pressure machines that would do a good job of work. Something with a big single cylinder between the frames will not be self-starting and may be slightly jerky at low speed, but it will work well nonetheless and the slow exhaust beats are a joy to hear. Less attractive is the sound of the magnificent raspberries blown when an Archangel safety valve blows off.

The technology of heating systems that require flames to be sucked past heating surfaces is quite extensive. We refer to them as 'internally fired'. You may hear the expression 'Smithies Boiler'. The actual boiler is smaller than the outer wrapper. A gas or spirit fire is located in the bottom of the firebox. The hot gases are sucked along the space between the two tubes, into the smoke box and up the chimney. There needs to be a source of energy to do the sucking. When lighting up, a small fan needs to be fitted to the chimney. Once there is some pressure on the clock, a blower valve is opened that sends a fine jet of steam out of it from inside. The electric fan is removed and this jet now sucks the heat along. Once the engine is running along the track, the exhaust from the cylinders will do the sucking. But I always like to keep the blower cracked a touch. An internally fired boiler is well suited to long continuous runs on a well-laid track. It is hard work to do constant shunting manoeuvres down at ground level with a loco that has one.

This is a somewhat simplified view of the subject (there are all sorts of alternative, internally fired boilers to be had), but such things are well documented – particularly in gauge 1 and gauge 3 practice – and so available for your further study. An Aster catalogue usually covers this well.

## COAL-FIRED DRAGONS AND OTHER BEASTS

The ultimate in realism is, of course, coal firing. The smell is magnificent and the whole feeling is just right. You would think that this is what everybody would aim for. Surprisingly, this is not the case. Whereas the model engineer, with his larger-scale engines, only has to concentrate on the great pleasure of driving them, many of us in the garden are more concerned with running a complete railway. The demands of maintaining steam with a tiny fire may not fit in with our aims of relaxing with a complete layout, together with shunting and running a service. It can be done with steam coal and it can be very rewarding. But maybe it is something to be considered at a later date, after we have some experience under our belt.

There was a time when driving very small coal-fired locos bordered on the miraculous. There were some model-engineered 0-gauge designs that required everything to be just right, and the driver to have uncanny intuition, to get a run out of. But to some, it was that very challenge that was the attraction. However, the world has moved on and it is now possible to get a 16mm or G-scale coal-fired engine that will look after itself for fifteen minutes without attention. Quite a lot of extremely high

*A coal-fired Penrhyn loco under construction. This has to be unashamed engineering. There is no room for short cuts here if it is to work and to be safe.*

*Walter Kolb built this impressive machine in G scale. (Photo: courtesy* Die Gartenbahn*)*

*This Funkey diesel is in 16mm scale and was built by Alan Walker. It is battery powered, but similar models have been built with genuine diesel-electric power.*

*Geoff Young produced this lovely little clockwork loco, and helped to keep an old tradition alive.*

quality engineering goes into them and this is reflected in the extra cost. But, once mastered, the driving experience is superb.

There has been a variety of more unusual engines used in the garden. Diesel-mechanical, diesel-electric and diesel-hydraulic systems have all been tried, sometimes on a small commercial scale. Early diesel-mechanical projects consisted of taking a small model aero engine and gearing it down to drive wheels. They could be noisy, smelly and difficult to start, but very enjoyable nonetheless. One variation I tried was a ducted fan loco that sucked air in at one end of a 'diesel' loco and blew it out the back. There have been a limited number of diesel-electric models commercially available.

Some of these are at the sharp end of technology and call for precise attention to detail before and after a run. But, especially when radio controlled, the driving experience can be tremendous.

Some enthusiasts still find spring drive (clockwork) a rewarding area to inhabit; others, myself included, have experimented with rocket propulsion. However, I must confess that my forays into this field have not always met with unqualified success!

*A gauge 1 DMU lurks unobtrusively on a siding. They are not the easiest of things to build from scratch and so are not a common sight on garden railways. (Photo: Geoff Culver)*

*For newcomers who want to get into larger gauges: a commercial 'Magic Carpet' powered wheelset, sold for G scale, has been extended to take 2½in gauge loco driving wheels.*

## BATTERY POWER

Battery-powered locomotives are very successful. The variety and size seem endless. I run small 7mm scale models on 00-gauge track using small batteries and revel in never having to clean the track to ensure good electrical contact. Indeed, that is one of the main advantages: instant running at the flick of a switch. There are also those little toy car conversions we spoke of earlier and the range extends thereafter right up to 3½in gauge locomotives that are powered by 12V gel batteries

The technology at its simplest comprises a battery, a motor and an on/off switch. The engine will only go in one direction but at least it is going. A cheap next step is to buy something called a double pole, double throw, centre off switch (DPDT). This is a three-position switch that gives forward, off and reverse. In truth, most of my own fleet is controlled like this because they run so slowly that I never felt the need for speed control. However, there are low-priced commercial bolt-ons available that will fit into a very small space. Battery-powered locomotives are naturals to have radio control fitted. They are made for each other; technologies marrying perfectly. Then, of course, there are the oddballs. I once built a small battery-powered, diesel-outline shunter. I adapted a sonic

*An unpretentious battery loco in 16mm scale. It happens to be made entirely of metal, but card, plastic-card or even thin plywood could have been used. There is a geared electric motor driving an axle. This is powered by a battery, controlled by a simple forward-stop-reverse switch.*

control system from a toy car to control it. Imagine my delight when I discovered that it would respond to a short rude word shouted at it, instead of the little clicker provided. I demonstrated this facility at an exhibition. It was surprising just how touchy some onlookers were. They just didn't appreciate a mechanical marvel when they saw it. Yes, this is still a hobby for individuals and experimenters.

---

## BATTERIES

If something is battery-powered, we can stick some ordinary batteries in and off it goes . . . unless the batteries are flat. It makes sense to use rechargeable ones. Nickel Cadmium (Ni-Cad) batteries are convenient replacements. Even better are Nickel Metal Hydride (Ni-MH). They are more environmentally friendly and give good service. Don't mix types or try to recharge non-rechargeable batteries. In fact, be organized about your batteries if you use a lot – particularly if you use them for radio control as well as traction. That way you will be spared the unwelcome surprise of opening up a battery compartment to find it all green and gungy . . . and possibly a wrecked mechanism as well. Battery charging isn't an entirely straightforward process. Some batteries need to be fully discharged before recharging otherwise they lose capacity. Fortunately chargers that do the thinking for us have removed much of the brain strain.

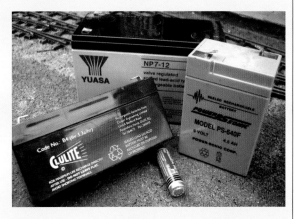

*Compact gel batteries are useful in larger models. An AA pen cell provides a comparison of size.*

*Four cells sit neatly into this 0.16.5 scale bogie wagon – to be covered by a tarpaulin.*

*A convenient battery format would be this little wallwart charger and four nickel-metal hydride batteries.*

Years ago, bigger batteries tended to be full of acid in liquid form and could be hazardous if knocked over. But now we have the pleasures of gel batteries, which are much more civilized. They also come in smaller sizes (sold for burglar alarms and the like) that will fit into useful little spaces.

There is a trade-off with batteries. The big gel batteries can be so heavy as to need a more powerful motor to power them, which in turn could call for a bigger battery. So we tend to use the more common pen cells or type 'C' or 'D'. Tables are available from manufacturers of current requirements of the current drain of differently rated electric motors but I tend to work on a trial and error basis. On a convenient shelf there is a box of different battery holders, batteries and plugs, and I simply fiddle with them until the loco runs well.

Model aircraft or racing car battery packs are worth looking at for particularly efficient operation.

*The author put together this distinctive coking-plant loco in plastic card. The main body houses a gel battery.*

*Most garden railways will benefit from having a simple, rugged battery loco. This weathered example was mostly home-made in brass, but there are many commercial kits available.*

A further advantage of the battery locomotive is that, once the chassis is up and running, the body that sits on top of it is merely cosmetic (as a poverty-stricken teenager, I made interchangeable bodies for the few working chassis I had). These bodies can be conversions, dreadful assemblies of bits of wood, superb card engineering, plastic creations, lovely metalworking and all points between. In these more hi-tech days, proper card modelling is largely a forgotten art but it still has its advantages. Go to the top of a multi-storey car park and drop a card locomotive body, an etched-brass one and a plastic one over the side. The card one survives best.

The outline can be anything you like. A simple battery locomotive outline can be made up with a few pieces of plastic card and items from the scrap box. A toy American lorry will provide many parts. Thereafter, we can increase the complexity up to the level of skilled metalsmithing to produce intricate steam-outline models. In other words, this is a hobby available to any skill level. The only limitation is the scope of your imagination. You can play your part in widening the range of garden railways or you can just enjoy the sheer pleasure of running trains.

*This modest conversion of a cheap 'Big Hauler' by Bachmann now runs off a gel battery in the tender. Even without any modifications, the satin black spray would have killed the shiny plastic look.*

*The loco peeking out on the right is a modified LGB. The one on the left is mostly card in construction. Both are battery-powered.*

*A lovely NER electric locomotive in 2½in gauge. Such things could collect juice from the track or be battery-powered – there is certainly plenty of room. (Photo: Geoff Culver)*

*An engine can be an artistic object in its own right. Although it is a functional machine, there is something about it that could produce a harmony of line, to be appreciated for its own sake.*

## THE BASIC INGREDIENTS OF A LIVE STEAM LOCOMOTIVE

OWAIN was drawn up to produce a reasonable scale model of a Vale of Rheidol locomotive, using mostly Merlin Locomotive Works standard parts, including their live steam cylinders. I was delighted when Messrs Roundhouse produced a delicious scale model in live steam, which does full justice to the majesty of the originals. Behind those very large side tanks lurks a fairly conventional, gas-fired locomotive.

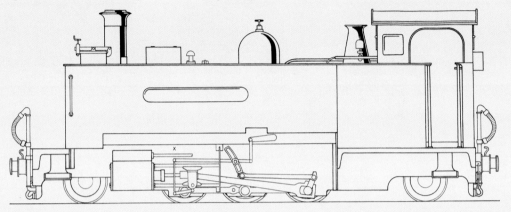

*Drawing: Judy Jones*

Those large side tanks would make excellent shielding for a meths-fired potboiler should such things be to your taste. But these days gas firing has come to predominate. Being a large model it would lend itself to coal firing, although the back (and maybe the cab roof) would have to be removable for access. If I were going to build this as a coal-fired model from scratch, I might well be tempted to use those big side tanks and the large cab to conceal an oversize firebox to make firing more stable.

The drawing shows the little pony wheels concealed inside the straight mainframes. But we have to be a bit pragmatic and have cut-outs so that these wheels can swivel to accommodate sharp curves. The cab roof has to be removable or at least capable of hingeing upwards to give access for the overscale gubbins that is concealed therein. Also, you can't scale nature. So a tiny steam whistle can only give a tiny 'peep'. There are designs for 'resonator' whistles that occupy a chunk of space and these sound a bit better. A lower-tech solution is to conceal a large over-scale whistle inside one of the side tanks. This gives a slightly better sound but still fails to capture the tingle of the real thing. The best solution I have heard is the cheat of having a sound unit play a digital chip through a speaker, controlled from the transmitter.

*Roundhouse models produced this superb commercial example of a V of R loco. (Photo: Gareth Jones)*

## SOMETHING MORE RADICAL

*Away from the mainstream there is so much yet to be tackled. The prairie dogs look askance at this pole-road locomotive.*

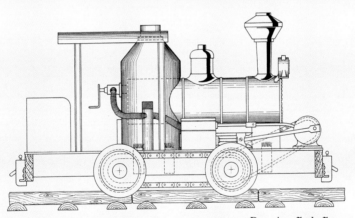

*Drawing: Judy Jones*

There are vast areas of locomotive design to be explored in model form. One unusual railway byway was the pole-road engine – built to run on broad gauge tracks where the rails were simply shaped tree trunks. The gauge could be quite broad but speeds were low, of course. Whitefish was my design for a practical working pole-road engine. A single commercial cylinder assembly drives an intermediate axle (layshaft). The double-stage chain coupling to the wheels allows for two lots of gearing down so the model runs nice and slowly – and has enough power to overcome the increased friction of the poles (I used distressed dowel). The layshaft can also have an optional extra. By removing a pin to a different location, the engine unit can drive a winch instead of the traction wheels. It can haul scale logs out of a forest using a wire made from an old bicycle brake (inner) cable. It can also haul the loco itself up a steep incline. A simple globe valve is the regulator and slip eccentric gear is once more employed. The design used spirit firing and there were wicks in the firebox and also another hidden in the smoke box. The wheels were old clothesline pulleys.

I am not suggesting that you should build one straightaway. Instead the design merely highlights that locomotive design can be amazingly diverse. Browse through photographs of New Zealand timber lokies and be prepared to be nicely shocked. When you start into garden railways, it will probably be along fairly conventional lines. But there is nothing to stop you branching out into the unknown.

# CHAPTER 7

# Rolling Stock

I could take the easy way out with this chapter and say that this can all be bought and illustrate it entirely with manufacturers' photographs. But that wouldn't really convey the sheer scope of the sub-

*A rather pleasing Japanese coach in gauge 1. (Photo: courtesy Aster UK)*

ject and they are already well covered in magazines, society journals and on the Internet. Although there is real satisfaction to be had from just going out and buying something, we need to think about some of the broader options. As with locomotives,

we can build, buy or adapt; and balance expenditure, ability and patience in the process.

Narrow gauge prototypes have an added complication. We could, for example, fit ten small slate wagons into one South African bogie coal wagon, despite them being to the same scale. The bulk and profile of narrow gauge are pretty diverse things. So it is sensible to think about the overall nature of the proposed railway before starting to collect rolling stock. Needless to say, commercial product ranges tend to be compatible within themselves.

## SIMPLE SCRATCHBUILDING

Scratchbuilding simple wagons is one of the most enjoyable things you can do. The entire workshop can fit inside a shoebox and the workbench can be

*Look at that gorgeous texture. Scratchbuilt by Eric Lloyd, it drips atmosphere.*

*A simple van in scribed ply with card strapping and details.*

an old tray. Cutting up little bits of wood with a junior hacksaw is a civilized occupation, as is gluing them together. A metal ruler marked with millimetres, and a metal square, take care of doing simple jobs accurately. Even if you are very new to it, given decent light to work in, you will be pleasantly surprised at how it falls together. You will have to buy in things like buffer couplings and wheels of course, but it is still an enjoyable and low-priced occupation. Be warned though: experience suggests that it is folly to believe you will just build one wagon to see what it looks like. I guarantee that you will be so pleased at producing your first home-built model that you will be unable to prevent yourself from building many more.

Lolly (popsicle) sticks have provided the material for many a wagon, and are worth buying in bulk. A small plan pinned to a flat surface is covered with a piece of plastic film. Pieces of wood are cut to length and then glued together, being temporarily held down with pins. Stripwood makes the strapping that turns the whole thing into a rigid, flat side. This is glued in place. There is an aesthetically pleasing quality to something that is obviously made up with separate planks, even if it is backed by plywood for additional strength. A complete van body can be made in a Saturday afternoon. The chassis can be made on a Sunday afternoon, thus – in my opinion – making for the perfect weekend. The chassis consists of stripwood glued together and maybe pinned. Axle guards, buffing gear, wheels and brakes are added. Superglue, to which Rocket powder has been added to make fillets, does the job quickly. Wherever possible, fine pins or even tiny screws should physically reinforce the glue. It

is essential that the wheels align accurately, so you will need a flat surface. A piece of thick glass is as good as anything else.

A van roof can be made in a variety of ways. A couple of layers of card, laminated together and painted with white glue, will be nice and rigid. It could be built up with strips of wood running lengthways and then sanded. Thin ply can be held in place with thick stripwood and elastic bands until the glue has set, or it can be made from thin metal sheet. When you get into the swing of things, it makes sense to build wagons and vans in batches. Make up a jig from offcuts of wood, so that you can just drop chassis strips in place to glue them together – indeed, for real mass production, make up little cutting jigs so that cutting whole batches of strips to the same length is quick and easy.

## KITS

The advantage of using a kit is that someone else has cut out the wood components properly and made sure that everything you need is in one box. The instructions can vary from splendid to the ones I describe as 'shedding darkness on the subject'. In the past there have been wagon kits that seemed to consist of a bit of tree, a penknife and a good luck card. But the world has fortunately moved on since then. So it may well be a good idea to start off with a wagon kit to get the feel of everything, and then use that experience to start batch building your own hand-made vehicles.

When you first open the box of a wooden wagon kit, you may well be disappointed. It seems a lot of

*It isn't such a big step from scratchbuilding a bogie van to tackling a simple coach.*

*This brickworks wagon was built from a Pretania Foundry kit, distressed somewhat and then painted in wet clay.*

money to pay for a few strips of wood and some anonymous-looking bits of metal. It seems a far cry from a plastic kit of a model aeroplane. But once you get going, this feeling will soon pass. You will begin to realize that someone has had to take the time to prepare all of the components accurately by hand so you can build a model that has the right feel to it. Following the instructions, glue and pin pieces of wood together. Sand or file some bits, and

you create something that is a delightful object in its own right. And whilst you are doing so, you are gaining experience that will enable you to scratch-build later on. You will see from many of the photographs that my preference is for the well-worn look. But clean is good too. I would urge that freight stock is painted in matt colours, but the weathering and distressing that I apply is not compulsory.

A variant of the wood kit is one where a basic wooden shell is built and then covered with vac-formed plastic sheets that have detail moulded on. This can offer instant ornate panelling and detail. Sometimes there is a faint rounding off of this detail

*Much more respectable is this 2½in gauge open wagon. The chassis was built from a GRS kit and Bill Basey made a body for it.*

*This Talyllyn railway brake van was built from one of those kits that start with a ply shell which then has a vac-formed laminate stuck on top to provide the fine detail.*

because of the moulding process. But in the larger vista of the garden, this becomes virtually invisible.

## LOADS AND LOADS

A useful practice, when you have completed an open wagon, is not to consider it finished until you have built a load for it. It may make sense to avoid loose coal or gravel on the grounds that it is always only one slight nudge away from a mess that has to be cleared up. A better idea is probably to get a block of wood to drop in the wagon and then glue coal or timber planks on top. But blocks of wood can be heavy. So an alternative would be a block of white expanded foam that has had a piece of thin ply glued on top, over which your dummy load is fixed. Flat wagons can have loads made up of blocks wrapped in crêpe paper and soaked in white glue. When painted a dull green, this looks like a tarpaulin covering – perhaps secured by brown thread. Needless to say, these drop-in loads can be interchangeable. They can also be hollow should you want to conceal batteries in them.

With vans there is less opportunity for interest-ing loads, but bigger batteries can be hidden. I still occasionally run my first 'serious' garden railway locomotive. It is a freelance Ffestiniog loco built in

1953 to run on two-rail track using a very big old motor. To run that off batteries these days requires a chunky 12V gel battery that takes up the entire interior of a sturdy box van. It isn't the last word in efficiency but it enables me to enjoy this very old friend in motion. You can also hide small batteries in vans or coaches to run working tail lamps.

One rather enjoyable sub-hobby revolves around that lolly-stick technology. Tiny – and somewhat quaint – wagons and coaches are put together from lolly-sticks and small bits of scrap wood. You need a razor saw, some sticks and the ability not to cut the ends off your fingers. Alternatively, there are small vehicles that embrace fine-scale modelling. For example, slate quarries in North Wales were overrun with tiny little playpen wagons that seemed to breed out of control. Such things can be built from plastic kits, and make up part of a very authentically modelled scene. I have found that some of these kits can become rather fragile over time, and need to be carefully looked after. More durable are kits moulded in glass-filled nylon.

## COUPLINGS

You should think about couplings for a moment here. In narrow gauge practice they vary a great

*Really tiny quaint vans built by a variety of methods. Building these can be a hobby all of its own.*

deal. Railways chose their own pattern and you can do the same. Typically there will be a centre single buffer with a coupling hook on top and the rolling stock can be linked together with simple three-link chains. This is fairly cost-effective and the wagons can be pushed around curves (provided that they are not too sharp) without derailing or wanting to climb all over each other. If you have started out with a typical commercial locomotive, measure the height of the centreline of the buffer above railtop level. Make a note of this, and in all subsequent additions to your rolling stock make sure that this buffer height remains the same.

Because of the diversity in the size and bulk of different types of rolling stock, it may pay to be practical and avoid mixing the sizes. A rake of small quarry vehicles looks nice behind a tiny engine. Ten bogie coaches look magnificent behind a South African Beyer-Garratt. Let's leave them each to their own devices; life is simpler that way. If you are modelling specific prototypes, you might well feel inclined to fit the correct style of coupling. Some wagons and coaches have semi-automatic chopper couplings for instance. The fine-scale modeller may wish to fit these. But if you are adding a new coach to your existing stock, it makes sense to fit it with your standard coupling so that it can be used. After all, this is exactly what would have happened in full-size practice.

*The technique of applying a rusty finish is described on page 131, but it particularly suits models of small iron vehicles. This one looks like it has just been rescued from a flooded mine.*

*Cutting and shutting is a useful tool. This open-tram coach was adapted from a spare Bachmann tram body.*

The cheapest coupling arrangement consists of two plain wood block buffers, a tiny cuphook and a chain. This works very efficiently and I had many happy years of such things. But they are lacking in appearance. On the other hand, there are all sorts of big plastic automatic couplings to be found on different ranges of commercial rolling stock, designed to be foolproof and rugged. The downside is that they may well be grotesque or oversize in appearance. The vehicles are kept at too great a distance apart to enable them to go round toy train curves. But they work well and you may conclude that you could live with the appearance if functionality is your priority.

US-style knuckle couplers lend themselves to model use particularly well and have a reasonable appearance. If you are modelling tiny vehicles that would normally have pin (use cut-down pop rivets) and link couplings, but you want automatic operation, use 00-gauge automatic couplings for an unobtrusive appearance. Actually, the old-type Triang/Hornby hook and bar couplings make quite a useful system for even the larger narrow gauges, if fitted to home-made extender arms.

Standard gauge stock will doubtless be fitted with correct buffers and use three-link or screwlink couplings, as per the prototypes.

*The agenda of the collector is different indeed. Things are kept very clean and in good order. Some collectors do not run some of their more precious stock. Keeping the box in good condition is equally important.*

# WHEELS

Like couplings, wheels come in a wondrous variety of patterns. The cosmetic appearance of the wheel – such as the diameter and number of spokes – is important for fidelity to the prototype, but the real nitty-gritty happens down where the wheel touches the rail. The profile of the wheel and the size of the flange can vary greatly. Very fine-scale wheels look the best but they may be a bit too fine to cope with the rough and tumble of life outdoors, especially in a narrow gauge environment where tracks twist and turn and may 'move' a little in changing conditions.

Some systems have really crude wheel profiles and enormous flanges to make for reliable running on very irregular track. LGB produced some real dinner plates at one time and they are still rather big now compared to other products. They won't run on the more delicate rail sections produced by other manufacturers. However, they work well and out in the garden this crudeness is much less obvious.

Whilst we should make use of whatever comes our way, given a choice, I would urge simplicity with bogies. If track is so bad that it requires a sophisticated sprung and compensated bogie to go round it, then I suggest that it is the track that needs time spending on it. I have one or two very old vehicles where the bogies are made from simple bent brass and have steel axles running in holes that are innocent of any bushing. They have given trouble-free service for decades. I don't claim that this is the best approach, merely that it works well. Live steam locomotives have enough weight to make the feel of sprung wheels seem attractive. There is something very satisfying about the way a properly sprung engine noses over pointwork. However, at one time I had two near-identical commercial live steamers that differed only in that one was sprung and the other was not. There wasn't a scrap of difference in how smoothly they ran on my railway.

Need I make the obvious point that any system using two-rail electrification must have insulation? Generally, metal-rimmed wheels run and sound a bit better on metal rails than plastic ones but it is not worth losing sleep over. For slow-running little trucks and engines, you can get away with using white-metal wheel castings and enjoy doing so. But they are not suitable for serious business.

Much of what we do in the garden is delightfully free from strict rules and regulations. But the back-to-back measurement of wheels is something we need to get right. Its name is self-explanatory, referring to the distance between the backs of wheels when mounted on an axle. For 32mm gauge track, the back-to-back is 28.5mm. LGB has a back-to-back measurement of 39mm for the

*Coach sides can be built up from individual pieces, which avoids trying to cut out windows accurately. You will see that the detail of the wheels is practically invisible.*

*For small layouts, the steam railmotor (known by various other names around the world) can be a useful complete train in a small space. This commercial example is in H09 scale.*

45mm gauge it runs on. This ensures both that the wheels roll nicely on the track and that the wheel sets will slide through the crossings and checkrails at points. Incorrectly spaced wheels are the cause of many derailments. Don't expect all of the small manufacturers to get it right all of the time. Always check. Any inexpensive calliper will do the job quite nicely, and it will find plenty of other uses too.

Those simple open wagons we spoke of are just a starting point. If we make them higher and put curved roofs on, we have box vans. I like to use real planks that haven't had the grain patterns sand-papered away. But there are plenty of alternatives. One approach, which is well worth exploring, is to make a box van shell in ply and then clad it in card upon which all the lettering has been printed on a computer.

*Rolling stock can be as challenging as you want to make it. This superb gauge 1 breakdown crane, with matching vehicles, can stir the blood in all of us. But more importantly it can get us out into the workshop, inspired to try it for ourselves. (Photo: Geoff Culver)*

## MORE PRACTICAL THOUGHTS

Plastic card is a particularly good medium to work in when building passenger stock, provided that common sense is used in making things rugged enough. One way to make passenger coaches is to take a long sheet of thin plywood and saw out all the window openings accurately, but this is not to be recommended to the inexperienced. An easier method is to use a single piece of Perspex as the basis of a coach side and then glue individual pieces of wood or plastic card on top, leaving openings that form the actual windows. There is no need for perfection, so don't worry if you can't cut a neat row of openings in a single sheet – I don't even try. My sole objective is to produce a model that looks right, without any unwanted wobbly bits. So I will go for whatever technique gives me that.

Rolling stock provides real possibilities for alteration and adaptation, offering plenty of scope for converting one scale model into something else. Quite crude toys can be turned into realistic models. Mostly it is simple cut and shut, and always great fun. On the other hand, when we get into standard gauge territory, a completely different approach is sometimes called for. This is a world where accurate modelling of fine detail is the norm – something is either right or it is wrong. It can be regarded as fine-scale indoor modelling moved out of doors. Fortunately, most of the technology for this is already well established. The only useful observation I can make is that the track needs to be in a safe and clean environment, well away from

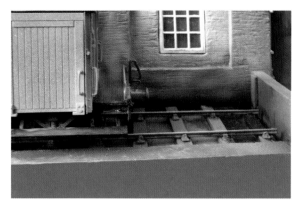

*And here it is with a small amount of tweaking and a drab paint job. Note the un-subtle buffer stop on the right, to prevent trains crashing to a concrete path at a critical location.*

earth falls and invading plant life. It is a real pleasure to watch a beautifully modelled and finely detailed goods train sweeping over points and out into the countryside – picking up mangled remains clogged with dirt is not.

Most of the above has been directed at narrow gauge, but things like 0-gauge fine-scale modelling have their own agenda. Wagon kits may well be plastic based in the first instance. For an active outdoor life I would be inclined to reinforce corner and edge joints with small fillets. Perhaps an open wagon could have a small block of balsa-wood filling the inside and be topped by a dummy load. If plastic buffers or wheels come with the kit then it makes sense to replace them with metal equivalents. Extra weight is worthwhile. Very light wagons in particular can be blown off the track even in a fairly moderate wind. Whatever scale/gauge combination you wish to work in, it is useful to have a short, very heavy train ready for instant use in poor conditions. Visitors do not always choose calm, sunny days.

Wagons and coaches made from exquisite etched-brass kits may also be fragile. You could think about extending the above principle a little further. I would recommend that you reserve your really accurate and fine-scale stock for running either in private or with trusted friends. But for visitors with an unknown provenance, perhaps run a less precious train. It is unlikely that anyone in a group of Scouts will pick up that your goods train

*A budget LGB box van of continental appearance.*

*A rake of four-wheelers in 0 gauge being built from vac-form kits. These will need beefing up before they are finished if they are destined for hard work in the garden.*

does not have the correct Glasgow and South Western brake van at the rear. They will be swamped by all the new sensations and images anyway.

The same may also apply to coaching stock. A rake of repainted 0-gauge Lima Mark 1s will make for an impressive train whilst your exhibition-quality Midland Clerestories stay out of harm's way. Besides, it is no bad thing to make your first train of the day up out of simple stock that won't suffer too much damage if it hits a frog sheltering in the tunnel. Although there are some budget 0-gauge vehicles available, building up long trains with them can be expensive. But don't worry about it for now. Buy what you can, when you can. The collection will build up with time. There are always plenty of second-hand supplies to be had. You might need to change wheels or couplings but that rarely presents a problem.

*Alternatively a plastic tipper can follow real practice, seen from time to time, and become a planter. If you want to be really cunning, cut a hole in the bottom of the body and run a tube down into soil concealed beneath the track. This gives real plants a more stable growing base.*

*As well as running, rolling stock can perform useful jobs in the garden. Some genuinely rusty steel tippers still have a role to play as line side accessories.*

I will conclude this chapter with a dose of reality. At the planning stage of your railway, you may well have mapped out lists of the rolling stock you would like to acquire. They will all have Acme couplings and they will all run on Roadrunner Perfectos wheels – while this is all very well in theory, the chances are that you will pick up odd bargains here and there and change your priorities as you go along. You will become pragmatic like the rest of us. Doubtless you will see an advert for some new kit that you don't need but can't resist. In narrow gauge practice in particular, you will find that one

*A Hornby 00 gauge pullman coach looks superb, but is perfectly usable out in the garden.*

*There is a whole world of interesting vehicles out there. These two gauge 1 wagons by Aster are a bit different from the more usual stock found on layouts. (Photo: courtesy Aster UK)*

vehicle isn't compatible with another or that something else just doesn't like a particular curve. Later on you may well be able to work these problems out for yourself. But for now, you will live with an eclectic mix of rolling stock. It isn't logical but it is enjoyable. Make sure that the back-to-back measurement of the wheelsets is accurate and that you convert to one sort of coupling, set at the right height. Then sit back and enjoy the quirks and idiosyncrasies of your railway.

# CHAPTER 8

# Buildings

It might be useful to remind yourself at this point that the garden gauges are seriously big. They need the size that a garden offers to be able to give of their best. The secret is not to be afraid of the size but to really enjoy it. Be bold. Don't make buildings and structures under scale. If you are worried about something being over-dominant, go for a model of a smaller prototype instead.

The track is pretty well resistant to all weathers. The locomotives and rolling stock generally live under cover when not in use. Your buildings and structures get the greatest hammering from the elements. So bear that in mind and proceed. It is common practice to bring model buildings indoors during the winter. I seem to be in a small minority that doesn't. This is for two reasons. First, my railway is intended for all-year use. Second, I found that moving and storing my buildings often did more damage than the weather. But that is just a personal preference.

Let us start our general overview with plastic kits intended for outdoor use. Although they will often be made in Europe, they are freely available in the UK and the USA. The plastic used will be really substantial and of a type that resists the effects of ultraviolet light. They will be models of European or US prototypes but many are easily converted to British appearance. Very often, just altering the pitch of the roof and cutting down the overhangs will make a dramatic difference. In the UK, some of these models will seem horribly expensive, but you can console yourself that you don't need many of them and, anyway, it is worth something to have attractive and low-maintenance structures.

Less ambitious than major conversions to plastic kits are minor tweaks and a conviction that you don't have to follow building instructions to the letter. Being flexible about mixing and matching kits

*A continental plastic kit of a 'house under construction'.*

can introduce some originality to your models. One of the drawbacks of the more popular kits is that one sees so many of the same structures, over and over again. This is more pronounced if they are left in the raw colours of the moulded plastic. Sympathetic painting can bring a more realistic feel to everything. For example, a railway often has its own house colours (literally!) for buildings. So if you have constructed all the elements of a station area, try painting all of the wood and metal areas in a single shade. A satin neutral green on bargeboards, doors, lampposts, seats and so on, will tie everything together that much better. This is a good rule to follow anyway but it is particularly useful with commercial plastic kits of buildings.

*Even as a newcomer to garden railways, start to record interesting buildings straight away. One day you may be grateful for them. They can be sketches, photographs or properly measured drawings.*

*Getting dimensions for a drawing can be made easier with a simple measuring stick. This one consisted of a piece of white plastic curtain rail, painted black at 12in (30cm) intervals.*

The good garden railway enthusiast will also scour jumble sales and car boot sales for children's toy buildings. There is a variety of houses, castles and the like that can be weathered and distressed nicely for our purposes. A plastic castle can be quickly 'ruined' with a few quick passes of a blow-lamp. And on the subject of children's toys, I am not going to tell you that Lego bricks, 'borrowed' from your children, can each have a face smeared with a hot knife before assembly, to give a nice stone wall when assembled.

## CONCRETE

Concrete is, of course, the best material for durability. There may not be much fine internal detail but archaeologists will ponder over your goods sheds in a thousand years from now. I divide these structures into two types. First, there are the solid castings. It doesn't take long to make a simple wood mould to cast a line side hut. Here I mention again the principle that has served me well over the years. I mostly cast my buildings with smooth faces. The mould is struck as soon as possible, when the concrete is still soft but can support itself. This gives a surface texture like cheese that is very easy to scribe stonework into quickly. Depending on the mix, the

*A substantial, chunky concrete building will be durable and can be put in some inaccessible corner and forgotten about. Incidentally, the old loco and wagon in this remote spot are bolted to the track to stop them being blown away. This simple, almost crude, cameo could stay unchanged for centuries.*

best time to do this is between four and eight hours after casting.

I find that a 4:1 mix of cement and sharp sand works well. It is slightly textured and it resists cracking. In a large structure I would incorporate some aggregate to increase the physical strength of the final lump. If you are feeling particularly confident, the best solution is to line the sides of the mould with a sand/cement mix but to fill the centre with aggregate-based concrete. This is a sort of variable mix that is applied a bit as a time, slowing filling the mould up. However, it isn't essential. I paint all newly cast mouldings in diluted waterproof PVA glue straight away. This seals the pores in the still damp structure. Two benefits flow from this – frost is resisted and less paint is needed. Indeed, if the first coat of paint is applied before the glue has dried, it bonds it nicely into the model and prevents paint flaking later on. If I want to incorporate a proper window or door into a solid cast building, I fix a thick chunk of wood behind the fitting. This assembly is then very lightly pinned to the inside of the mould, just enough to hold it in place when the concrete is poured in, and no more. When the mould is struck, it leaves the fitting trapped in the concrete.

In a very large chunky casting, the cost of sand and cement can be reduced by casting a couple of breezeblocks or bricks into the heart of the moulding. Although these can be phenomenally heavy, it doesn't matter if something is being cast in place. But if it has to be carried or lifted up high, thermalite blocks or even polystyrene foam could be substituted.

The other type of concrete building is where individual walls are cast and they then form a 'kit' to assemble the model. You will often see this used in commercial model villages where the structures are extremely large. In my garden is a large ruined abbey, which disguises a wild natural corner (*see* page 158). I made the moulds on a substantial plywood baseboard and then put in timber strips to delineate the edges and window openings. This could be scribed in stone before striking the mould. The casting is about 1in (35mm) thick and I incorporated several non-ferrous reinforcing rods, although I am not sure that they were essential. I also cast in some holes at either end for fitting locating pins when I came to join the whole thing together. Two sides and two ends were cast, of course. I wanted to incorporate the remains of an ancient gothic window in one end. To achieve this I made a mould in plywood and then cast it in lead. The four walls were erected with brass dowel in the locating holes. Other than that, they were simply stuck together with white PVA glue, which proved to be surprisingly effective in this application. However, the bases of the walls were concreted into the uneven ground anyway, so the whole thing is totally solid. The areas inside and out were then planted with low-growing green things, but mostly left for nature to take over. We shall return to more ambitious concrete practice towards the end of this chapter.

## POTTERY BUILDINGS

I don't pretend to understand the subject well, but have evolved a useful rule of thumb. A pottery object that has a shiny glaze should be more resistant to frost damage than one that has not. But I am always aware of this being a possible hazard. So I would swill some dilute white glue around the inside of any pottery item and then fill the thing full of concrete. For an unglazed pot, I would dampen it first and then paint on waterproof white glue, inside and out. This is a time for a good jabble with a stiff brush. I might even be tempted to paint the model with a basic colour whilst the glue is still wet. This is a gloriously messy procedure but it does make the thing more resistant to water, and hence the risk of frost damage.

There are sources of pottery buildings, often with a British appearance, which are aimed directly at the garden railway enthusiast. If you are short of time or modelling skill, they can provide an attractive way to introduce buildings at an early stage.

## WOOD AS A BUILDING MEDIUM

Wood has an annoying habit of rotting, and plywood is partial to falling to bits. But there are ways to get round this. To make a building in plywood, I would cut the panels out and then 'fire' all exposed edges with a blowlamp, something we discussed earlier. White glue is then jabbed into the warm wood and the pieces assembled with brass pins, which hold things together whilst the glue sets. Don't worry if the building becomes smeared with

*A commercial pre-cast building is painted to be believable. Suitably sealed with white glue first, it is frost resistant.*

gluey charcoal, as it makes a kind of well-sealed homogeneous whole. Be warned that this is just as messy as putting glue and paint on to pottery buildings. I used to engrave stone courses with a vibrating electric engraver but it is tough on the wrists. I get better results by sticking lots of little snapped-off pieces of thin wood in place as separate 'stones', but it is a slow process.

For a brick finish I score horizontal lines and then tap every small vertical with a pin hammer and screwdriver. My preference is to use fibreglass castings or plastic mouldings for windows and doors. Thin, transparent plastics tend to go milky after a couple of years but genuine Perspex is much better behaved. Best of all is real glass. If you are worried about the fragility of it, let me reassure you. Our buildings are so well built that, if you have an accident that breaks the glass, the chances are that this will be the least of your problems! To get this real strength, I prefer to line the whole of the inside wall with a single piece of really thick glass rather than using individual slips of glass in each window. In fact, with buildings that have a large window area, I often start with the piece of glass and build the

*This ambitious signal box is built around a plate-glass frontage, covered with different types of cladding. This gives strength to those fragile-looking windows.*

*In fact the detail can get very small indeed.*

*A substantial timber-built building, with individual wooden 'stones' cladding the outside.*

*Going in a little closer, we see the scope to enjoy fitting a detailed interior.*

detail up on that. This is particularly good for signal boxes or shop windows.

Whilst it adds realism to have an occasional door or window opening, my suggestion is that it is better not to, as all sorts of tiny creatures crawl inside and make their homes there. There is a surprising test for how well a building is sealed, and that is to tap it. If it has good joints everywhere and is well sealed, it rings like a bongo drum. Although there are plenty of ingenious ways of adding detail to a building, making it durable should first and foremost be our main preoccupation.

## SLATE ROOFS

To put a slate roof on a building is cheap and easy but time consuming. The structure of the roof is made from thin ply, with those edges heat-treated again. It is then liberally painted with white glue *both* sides and pinned or glued in place. I have found that, with the exception of the real thing, the most durable 'slates' are made from absorbent card, the stuff you get on the back of reporters' pads. This material sucks in white glue to become a very strong and weather-resistant end product. Although you can cut slates in long strips and overlap them, a better effect can be achieved by sticking one slate on at a time. Make sure that the roof is marked with plenty of horizontal lines first; there is nothing worse than sloping rows. The occasional chipped or slipped slate is acceptable but it is best not to overdo it. This can be a monotonous task and I find that the best way round it is to do a few slates over a short period and then go off and do something more interesting instead. Next time I am passing the model, I stick a few more on. It is surprising how quickly the job is done without any real effort. I find that it is the cutting out of the slates that takes the time. So I have a little cutting board,

*Sunrise over a* very *large wood-built mill building. It is a functional structure that contains an electrical distribution point and a water pump (ex-washing machine) for the adjacent water wheel.*

*An ornate goods shed built in timber with card slates.*

a knife and a steel ruler close to my desk. That way, when I am writing away, I can take a few minutes off to cut a few more slates.

It is possible to buy vac-formed plastic slate roofing for models, but I have found my treated card to be just as weather resistant over the years. However, vac-formed sheets of slates, tiles, bricks and stones can be a useful resource. They do need painting to protect them from ultraviolet light, which may cause brittleness with time.

## OTHER MATERIALS

If Welsh slate railways are to your taste, and you enjoy a modelling challenge, then consider building them out of real slate. This will cut in a bandsaw and will snap and cleave like the real thing. It is time-consuming to glue all the little pieces together with waterproof PVA or similar around wood formers, but the end results can be exceptional.

It comes as a surprise to some to learn that expanded foam – as in white ceiling tiles and insulation boards – can be a useful material for buildings. Walls can be engraved into stone coursing and then the individual panels glued together with clear silicone sealant. I like to push a few wooden pins in for mechanical strength as well. Bamboo skewers or toothpicks are a useful resource here. Paint the buildings in a mix of white glue, perhaps with a little filler paste mixed in. This will bond the surface and prevent flaking. Stick to using water-based paints unless you enjoy the spectacle of dissolving models. A denser form of thin plastic can often be found underneath a pizza, and in all manner of food trays. This carves, embosses and scribes very well and makes for a good textured cladding material. It is durable out of doors when fixed to a rigid carcass and painted over.

*Alan Walker made this station building from individual slate blocks and roof slates. (Photo: Alan Walker)*

*This overgrown shack was made from pieces of white plastic foam. The roof uses an offcut of twin-wall plastic sheeting.*

*How about a burnt-out engine shed? This is actually made from chips of wood, glued over a cardboard shell. Given enough white glue and paint, it has enjoyed a surprisingly long life out of doors.*

*Dave Lomas made this station building from resin castings he made, using Jig-Stones rubber moulds (see page 124). (Photo: Dave Lomas)*

# A SAMPLE SMALL BUILDING

Instead of just listing materials, let me run through making a little line side hut. Cut the four walls out of exterior-grade ply. You aren't going to see the thickness of this so you can use chunky shuttering ply as something that is economical and durable. We will want to cut a door and window opening somewhere. There is no need to drill holes to insert a saw blade for the window opening. We can cut a line in from the side with a jigsaw. We will also cut

That simple hut can be expanded to form more complicated structures. Here, a larger station building is under construction. Like many of my models, it uses commercial plastic window frames.

A doodle of the front of a permanent way hut.

This eventually translates into the simple model I have been building in words.

a piece for the floor and a ceiling. With a blowlamp, 'fire' all the raw edges of the ply pieces so that they are well charred. Whilst the wood is still warm, paint white glue over everything. It is messy but worth it. Remember, with plywood, it isn't the wood that fails, it's the glue that holds the laminations together.

When these panels are well dried, glue them together and fit the floor, using waterproof white glue. You will notice that I make a lot of use of this, which is why I stress buying it in large tubs from a bulk supplier. You can glue a commercial door and window moulding in place (having cunningly cut the openings to fit). They can be set in place with slow-drying epoxy-resin. The window will need glazing. The most easily obtained material is transparent plastic of some sort. It cuts easily and is cheap. But it does discolour over the years. If you can use genuine Perspex then so much the better. Best of all is real glass. Buy cheap and nasty pictures in jumble sales. There will be a sheet of thin glass and also four pieces of interesting sections of wood that will always find a use. Thin glass is easier to cut than thick. Incidentally, a glazier once told me that glass is easier to cut if you paint a little methylated spirits on it before scribing. I have no idea why it works but it seems to.

There are plenty of commercial window mouldings available. Before they came on the scene I used to keep an eye open for rectangular plastic or metal mesh that could be adapted. For a specific need I have made up a single window frame in brass and then produced a mould in re-meltable rubber. Pure resin castings are fragile in thin section so, for window frames, I use a car filler paste to make my castings. Doors can be bought or are fairly easy to make anyway.

To clad the building, break up small pieces of thin balsa wood in your fingers. It will naturally want to snap in long flat pieces. Start by gluing on lintels over the doors, the windowsills and the framing stones around the doors and windows. Then glue in matched-up corner stones. The remainder of all the cladding can be done with smaller stones. Don't try to squash them too close together and keep the courses level. Leave to dry and then paint the entire shooting match with more white glue. This will sink into the absorbent balsa wood and everything will harden to a completely integrated shell.

Glue the false ceiling in place. For the roof, I like to cut and fold up a piece of aluminium. It is bedded in silicone sealant and secured with brass pins. Roof tiles are glued in place with PVA, starting at the bottom and working upwards, keeping things level. The grey board on the backs of sketchpads is fine. Along the top I glue some folded capping tiles. Some people make the capping strip out of a piece of brass or aluminium angle. Small birds like to perch on buildings and, with time, their claws damage a card strip. Give the whole lot a glue seal and then we are ready for painting.

Start by coating the entire structure with some pale grey matt acrylic, from a bathroom paint sampler pot. Give the stones a coat of matt dark grey paint (woodworking undercoat is fine) on their tops, leaving the lighter grey showing through in the crevices. Remember all those framing and edging stones? Paint them in a slightly different colour for emphasis. After that it is just a question of taking a small paintbrush and going over the stones one by one, painting them in *very* slight variations of the main colour. We don't want it to look like a toy fort. The door and window are painted in a faded variation of your chosen colour and the roof slates a medium blue/grey. Again, you can go over a few individual slates in slightly different tones of the main colour. This all helps to make the building really 'sing' with realism.

If you want to add bargeboards, guttering and downpipes, do so. But you must remember that, with distance, detail is soon lost. So it isn't compulsory, especially if it is in the background. It is more important to blend the building into the landscape. If this is your first attempt at making a building yourself, it may all sound a bit complicated. But it really isn't. It is cheap and surprisingly quick to do. You have got a building that is unique to you. What is encouraging to know is that even the most complicated buildings usually turn out to be no more than lots of little boxes joined together. One unlikely option is to make a small goods shed with a hinge-up roof. It can be used to store pegs for a clothesline.

## SIMPLE FUNCTIONAL BUILDINGS

Buildings can be much more than merely decorative. For example, an open-fronted concrete building with a metal roof can house a small toy steam stationary engine, rescued from the attic. With a few cosmetics added, it can form the heart of a small working engine house with steam coming from a proper chimney. There is something quite satisfying about having a little bit of working steam alongside the line. If you are entirely non-technical, try a small concrete model of a traditional lime kiln with a small round tin in the base. Fill it with sand and a little white spirit then drop a couple of twigs on. When lit, it will smoke gently.

## GROUPING

As well as the usual railway buildings and an occasional cottage, we can start to think about grouping buildings together to form something that suggests a model village. A collection of black and white (or brown and white) timber-framed buildings is an attractive addition to a garden railway. The structures can be made in a variety of ways. One is to build the timber frame first and then infill with little panels of heat-sealed ply. An easier alternative is to make the walls in that ply and then stick thin framing on. This is a fascinating hobby in its own right and visiting such villages (Weobley is a particular favourite of mine) for research, is a delightful

*Here is a full-blown brickworks, based on a sketch that I made many years ago. It can actually fire scale bricks.*

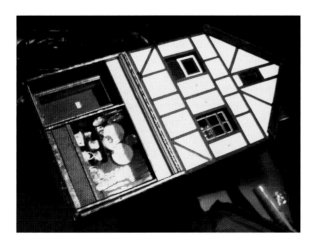

*This low-relief china shop is based on a wood box with a piece of plate glass in front covered with detail . . .*

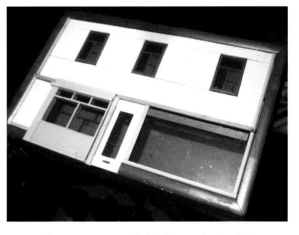

*. . . and here we see a part-finished example of a similar technique.*

*The low-relief principle has been taken to extremes with this brewery front. Again, its main component is a large piece of glass.*

occupation. You may come across models of timber-framed buildings commercially cast in concrete in roughly G scale. Enjoy giving them a coat of dilute white glue and then painting them. For realism, don't make the windows silver. Paint them in a gloss dark green and, in a top corner of each little pane, dab a rough spot of bright grey/green, which you will find is easier on the eye.

In the larger scales, there is extensive scope for adding details, such as properly filled shop window displays. This is mostly a world of making things from the scrap box. A broken figure can be used to make a display mannequin in a clothes shop window. This is pure modelling at its most informal.

## INDUSTRIAL BUILDINGS

I have gained notoriety for industrial modelling. Heavy industry provides the setting I want to run my trains through. I enjoy the modelling challenge and the drama of it all. It took me a long time to become confident enough to build really large structures. I was worried that they might over-dominate the garden and hence I produced under-scale things that were out of proportion to the trains. But I discovered that I was wrong. Large buildings, realistically set into the landscape, can have a 'rightness' about them. One example is a battery of coke ovens for a steelworks. In the workshop its 6½ft (2m) length and sheer bulk seemed overwhelming. When it took four men to carry it to its location my heart sank. But now, set in its

*Examples of brick and stone carving in plywood. This extreme close-up shows the value of getting the basic colour and texture right. In the case of the wall in the lower photo, even the door is merely carved in and painted.*

rightful place, it looks at home. As well as housing a concealed bulkhead light containing a 60w red fireglow bulb to cast a suitable glow, it contains a small disco fog unit. Thus splendid clouds of steam erupt on command and at night the sight is suitably heroic.

If you want some gentle industrial interest to give a purpose to the railway, you can do better than just a vague industrial plant next to a siding. Make a point of learning all about a specific industry. A small brickworks would have had its own equipment and wagons. Even if your aims are modest, enjoy modelling something original or seeking a specialist supplier. For example, I have found the catalogue of Pretania Foundry very inspiring, although often underscale for G or 16mm. Much

*The basic station building shown in an earlier photograph is now properly bedded into the landscape and is awaiting completion.*

*The sort of 'building' that is hard to define but great fun to make. This ruined boxcar has been satisfactorily invaded by greenery.*

*At the opposite end of the spectrum we can enjoy this substantial building at Holyhead at a dockside location on a 2½in gauge railway. (Photo: courtesy Gauge 3 Society)*

*Early morning at the model village of Bourton-on-the-Water. The real limestone is weathering and mellowing perfectly.*

of what goes into your garden railway may be very similar to other layouts. But with buildings in particular you can make an individual statement and broaden the base of the hobby for everyone else.

As with your own home, it pays to stay ahead with maintenance. Go round your building stock in springtime and just tidy things up. Even if a coat of paint is still intact, after a couple of years it may well have gone drab, so freshen it up anyway. Check your chimney pots for suicidal tendencies. And whilst you are at it, enjoy doing so.

## THE MODEL VILLAGE APPROACH

Perhaps the most impressive form of model building may be found in the true 'model village' approach, where it is the buildings that are the main attraction and the railway is almost secondary to that. We all know about commercial model villages (which can mean model towns and bits of cities as well), with their large buildings that you can walk around – often on footpaths disguised as model roads. These can be beautifully created works of art, like the one in Bourton-on-the-Water, England. On the other hand, they can be tacky, overcrowded and jumbled. But they can all teach us about the finer art of making more advanced model buildings. They are usually to a large scale that suits our garden gauges nicely.

The Bourton model village, mentioned above, uses hand-carved local limestone as the basic material – the end result is wonderfully sympathetic and it mellows beautifully with age. If you can

*Warm Cotswold stone has a real magic to it. It looks good in any light.*

obtain suitable material, it is possible to learn to work a soft sandstone or similar.

Given patience, working in slate is slightly easier. The fact that it will split well is no secret but you will also be pleasantly surprised by how easily it will saw and drill. And you don't have to live near slate

*For less challenging craftsmanship, imaginative use of concrete in a model village setting can be attractive.*

*Advanced concrete techniques can produce some very pleasing results.*

waste tips to get some useful bits. Broken roof slates (provided they really are made of slate) are quite thick and can be snapped and sawn to form individual blocks. Although it seems longwinded, building a concrete shell (or a thick ply inner carcass) and then cladding it in individual pieces of slate produces a magnificent feel of reality. They can be bedded in a 4:1 mix of sand and cement, a

## SOURCES OF INSPIRATION

Here are some examples of interesting buildings that have inspired me, when building my garden railway. There is so much to choose from: so much that can be modelled – and all waiting for you.

*My favourite American station: in Jim Thorpe, PA.*

*Brecon's canal basin. The vernacular cottages are new but the white tollhouse is original.*

*A long-disappeared station in Pembrokeshire. The photo gives so much atmosphere and detail.*

*The old station building at Llanfair Caerenion.*

*The mellow remains of Nevada City.*

## SOURCES OF INSPIRATION *continued*

*The old Corris station at Machynlleth – now isolated in an industrial estate.*

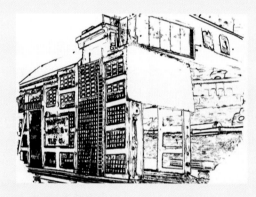

*A sketch of a brickworks.*

*A study of canalside houses near Neath: a favourite haunt of mine.*

*A lovely little shelter on the Welshpool and Llanfair railway. A full-size copy of this would make an excellent garden shed.*

*An old ironworks, where the bellows were powered by a splendid waterwheel. This is the sort of building that would make a lovely model.*

modest dollop of white glue and a dollop of black kiddies powder paint to take the rawness off the white colour.

We have already looked at the basic casting of buildings in concrete. With the model village perspective, we then turn to more ambitious techniques. Moulds are made for individual walls, complete with window and door openings. Finer detail may be made up of smaller castings glued on. With a bit of planning, the most complicated building is possible. It makes sense to use cement tints to colour the actual material and so cut down on later painting/maintenance. Best of all, go and visit as many model villages as you can. Take plenty of film (or digital memory) with you. Even 'unsuitable' model villages will provide a huge amount of inspiration. It broadens your whole perspective on the subject of buildings for your garden railway.

## USING COMMERCIAL BLOCKS AND BRICKS

From time to time, various commercial products that supply building blocks appear. A typical example might be packets of ready-made 'stone' blocks that fit together. You can make up your own structures out of these. It can be an expensive way of doing things but it is clean and simple. A cheaper alternative might be to buy rubber moulds and cast your own walls and components in resin. 'Jig-Stones' originated in the UK but are now based in the USA. I got a set of overscale block moulds from Arquetec some time ago. They may not be available now, but variations of such things seem to crop up from time to time.

Back in the 1950s there was a much-loved system called Brickplayer. This consisted of real, but overscale, small bricks and fittings. You put these together with a water-based paste to assemble buildings. To dismantle them, they were soaked in hot water. A building made of these today looks a bit crude but it has an aesthetic appeal all of its own.

A useful alternative is to make your own kit. For natural stone blocks, make up your own masters from bits of trimmed stone or even broken quarry tiles. Make up some sort of containing box and then pour hot-melting rubber compound (available from hobbies shops) over them, to form a thick rubber mat. When cool, pull the compound out and turn it over. Extract your originals and then place it back in the tray, face up. Then, whenever you are doing any cementing jobs, just trowel a tiny bit into the voids in the moulds. Over time you can build up a decent store of them, without any real cost. A stronger alternative would be to cast your blocks in resin. Again, it is a laborious job to specifically cast blocks, but it is a useful thing to keep going in the background to use up dregs.

When you have enough blocks to build a section of natural stone wall, the next stage would be to glue them together and complete it. Then re-use the hot-melt rubber to make a mould of the completed section – and cast further copies. Do not be tempted to use ordinary plaster out of doors. Despite all the sealing and painting you care to throw at it, it eventually dissolves back into the earth whence it came.

The whole subject of buildings for garden railways can be as simple or as complex as you want to make it. Somewhere in the middle comes the sort of layout that features the appropriate railway buildings and maybe a cottage or two. But, if you have an inclination for something more ambitious, then here is an opportunity to enjoy the building process and to paint three-dimensional pictures of sights now long gone. As with everything else connected with a railway in the garden, it is very much a matter of expressing personal choice and inclination.

# CHAPTER 9

# Painting

Garden railways call for a whole variety of painting techniques – some well established and others downright weird! So perhaps we should start by exploring familiar territory. Advice on painting small models seems to consist of carefully applying several thin coats using high-quality brushes and patience. In most cases, the tried and tested techniques still work best. My only personal observation is that an unsteady hand gets better results if it is supported at just the right angle by a block of wood or similar. There is more control over a beginner's brush if just the wrist does the moving, rather than the entire arm. Likewise, using a larger brush where possible will provide greater stability.

Locomotives and rolling stock tend to be large objects, so it helps to use a bigger brush. One tip for getting an even flow of enamel paint on to a larger area is to use lighter fuel as a thinner. Buying a lining pen and learning to use it is an option. One

*It is amazing how much brush control improves as soon as the hand is supported properly.*

*It is better to do a simple paint job well than a difficult one badly. The brown parts were done with a car aerosol and the black bits used a spray of satin black. Other colours were put in by hand and the boiler bands are polished brass.*

thing I can't do well is neat lining or lettering by hand. So I don't try. I take the view that no lining is better than wobbly lining but, if you have the patience, applying neat lines of paint is a skill that can be learnt.

Whilst you should *never* buy cheap brushes there is no real need to buy exotica either. As well as model shops, you may also find something you like in office and art shops at a reasonable price. Although the conventional wisdom is that brushes should be carefully cleaned in thinners after every use, wiped dry and carefully stored flat, I just give them a quick slosh in white spirit, and then toss them into a flat tray that has about an inch of water in it. There might be a dozen brushes floating there at any one time. For the next job I just grab a suitable one, possibly dip it in white spirit, give it a quick dry on a smooth cloth, and then get back to work.

However, if you are looking for an easy way to make three-line boiler bands, stick some brown plastic parcel tape on to a piece of glass. Paint it the background colour and leave to dry. Then rule lines with a black biro at random and spray with a matt varnish to seal. When this is dry, take a steel ruler and a scalpel and cut out strips so that you have the black line with a line of colour either side. With a scalpel blade, lift the strip and drape it around the boiler, securing it with a little Evostik.

## TRANSFERS

Fortunately there are commercial sources of transfers (decals) available that cover a wide range of applications. You can buy softening solutions to allow a carrier film to drape neatly over rivet heads, as well as fixatives. You can also get lining transfers applied for you commercially. Waterslide transfers are printed on to a thin transparent carrier film and will curl up nicely when soaked in a saucer of warm water. Just at the right moment, the loosened transfer is slid off its piece of backing paper and into place. It might try to crinkle up on itself but if you can slide it directly off the backing sheet straight on to the job this minimizes the risk. Dab the surplus water drops off with a tissue, and then make sure it is in the right place and correctly aligned. Leave it for a few hours to dry before giving a quick spray with some sort of matt sealant.

That carrier film can be quite obtrusive at times. A bad transfer might be one that says L N E R – with long spaces between the letters. It would look a bit better if those individual letters were cut out in small rectangles and applied individually. But that does call for accurate alignment. One dodge is to put a strip cut from a lo-stick Post-it-note on the location to act as a straight edge – perhaps with some pencil marks to indicate spacing.

One particularly nice form of transfer is the spirit-fixing type: 'Methfix'. This leaves no carrier film and positions can be adjusted slightly. But these have a limited availability.

Rub-on dry transfers leave no film either but these have the drawback that you have to be particularly exact in your lining up. There is no possible adjustment. If it has gone on slightly crooked then it has to be carefully scraped off and done again.

Traditionally, transfers used to be fixed with varnish. It takes a bit of practice to use just the right

*With various weathering techniques, brushes tend to be abused. It makes sense to keep a couple of good ones for decent jobs, and cascade the rest down.*

amount as an adhesive, and not to make a mess outside the transfer area. I have had quite a few failures over the years. But this may have been due to the fact that huge numbers of transfers of this type were made long ago and they still occasionally turn up for sale cheap: cheap because they have become extremely brittle with age. But it could just as well have been due to my own incompetence.

> When lettering stock with transfers bought in an office suppliers or art shop, there are a couple of common mistakes. Real railways very rarely use gold paint. It weathers badly and is drab. Instead the tendency was to use 'signwriters gold'. This is creamy beige with a faintest hint of pink mixed in. The real eyesore though is when you see ornate letters where all capitals are used. It is bad sign-writing practice and rarely used in the full-sized world.

## 'SCALE' PAINTING

There are two ways you can think about the paint finish of our models. The first is to treat them as objects in their own right. They are painted in the correct colours with as good a gloss finish as you can achieve or buy. You see them run exquisitely through their surroundings: artefacts that delight the eye. The alternative is to regard them as canvasses on which to paint realism. This doesn't mean simply splashing matt black paint on as some sort of weathering, but to use scale colour. We all know that grassy hills appear blue with distance. But colours start to recede at much closer distances than that. The trouble is that our brain automatically compensates for it. This is why a beautifully shaped black plastic engine can look so toy like. The black is too dense and the shine is too great. If we want realism in the wider sweep of the garden then we have to paint, according to the artist's adage, what we *see* and not what we *know*.

We may know that a black engine is painted gloss black but, even from a modest distance, what we actually see is a very dark warm grey with a dull sheen. Pure white becomes a pale grey. Indeed, all colours soften: just like turning the saturation down on a colour TV. This has nothing to do with weathering or variable light. This is just a simple

fact of physics. We can superimpose the dirt and age, but getting gentle versions of the correct colour is what gives the correct basis for realism.

The colour of a plastic moulded railway coach may well look rather fierce at first sight but when you think about it, the main culprit is the shiny roof. Going over that with a couple of slightly different washes of matt dark grey will transform the whole appearance straight away. If the black ends of the coach are similarly painted, those shiny sides will suddenly appear to be much more 'right'. Dull down the underframes as well and the object will be transformed from a plastic model into something that convinces the eye. The white colour of a coach roof was achieved by using a lead-based paint, which weathered extremely quickly. So, what with one thing and another, pure white is best avoided for such things.

One of the most overworked clichés in print is that 'weathering should be applied judiciously'. Unfortunately it happens to be true. Masterly understatement works best. My railway has a lot of heavy industry on it so the crud is thicker than it would normally be. Take an aerosol of matt 'earth' colour, as sold for military modellers, and give the underframes and wheels a very faint whiff. This instantly kills the shiny plastic. It also works well for model road vehicles. An equally slight wafting of matt dark grey from above will help to make it less garish. Incidentally, if you are modelling diesel locos or converting a road vehicle, cut out a couple of shapes that match the area covered by windscreen wipers from a Post-it note. When you spray a faint weather whiff all over, the cleaned area of screen, caused by the paper being used as a mask, looks nattily realistic.

However, if you have just spent a lot of money on a shiny new locomotive, you may not want to cover up that beautiful factory finish. So it may be that, even if you decide you want to join the 'realistic railway' school, you may accept the convention of having immaculate trains running. I would not dream of making any value judgements about the various approaches. This is a great hobby in all its guises.

For painting freight stock, buildings and structures, I like to use bathroom acrylic paints (or masonry paint) in sample pots. This gives me soft colours, cheapness and outdoor durability. If a

*This van started out as a cheap toy. However, the weathering transforms it into a model. For the perfect appearance, the tyres should be lightly filed away at the bottom so that they have that slight flat area where they touch the road.*

mistake is to be made, the most likely is that things will be painted too dark. Take a look at professional architectural models. They may be simplified but they often have a realism that comes from light, restrained colours.

## SPRAYING

If you are an airbrush wizard already then you need no further guidance from me. If not, there are some simple techniques you can use to serve the garden railway. With some reservations, the aerosol cans from an automotive supplier can be used. They usually deal a splendid hand in fumes so try to use them out of doors but be aware that cold and damp weather can affect the spray finish. What we need is the Peter Jones hi-tech spray booth. This consists of a large cardboard box turned on its side, flaps open. A hair dryer will blow out any dust and warm the inside. But the really neat trick is to fill a hot-water bottle and wrap it in a plastic bag. This keeps the inside of the box warm and dry for several hours and really gives a coat of paint a good start in life. An offcut of polythene sheeting can be rolled down over the now-closed flaps to keep any dust out.

Cellulose aerosols attack existing enamel paint finishes and also some types of plastic. It is sometimes possible to minimize the latter by making the first few coats just the faintest of dustings, sprayed from a distance, so that the paint droplets are virtually dry by the time they hit the plastic. Leave them to harden off and then they can act as a barrier to slightly heavier coats later. There are some water-based aerosols to be had from DIY stores but I have found them to be rather coarse. However, model suppliers offer high-quality enamel sprays in matt, gloss and satin. From automotive suppliers it is possible to get plastic-bumper sprays for cars. In particular they often come in a couple of realistic dark greys or dull black. They stick particularly well to plastic out of doors.

If you spray cellulose paints in particular on a damp day, as mentioned, it 'blooms' – gives a flat uneven finish. Given a bit of practice, you can make use of this. For example, if you have a bit of garish cement in your rock faces, spray it lightly with an aerosol of a warm light-green colour on a really damp day. This produces a much flatter finish that looks natural – and will flatten off completely in a month or so. If you can't wait for a damp day, spray the paint with the tin in one hand and a small water bottle spray in the other.

Also on the subject of spraying, it is worth noting that simple electric spray guns for doing large areas have come on a long way since the crude spatter-and-drip gadgets of yore. They are not really suitable for doing models but have many timesaving uses in the garden. Some versions will now handle thinned smooth masonry paint and bathroom acrylics. Moreover, the prices have reduced in real terms, thanks to the inexorable march of Far Eastern technology. The best sort to have is one where the compressor is in its own little box and the spray gun is at the end of a hose. You get a more powerful motor and less arm ache that way. But even a modest integrated spray gun has its uses.

The height of luxury is a big, shiny yellow compressor on wheels and a professional spray gun. But it is quite possible to manage without. Whatever gear you use, spraying should be done in a well-ventilated area – and there is nothing more ventilated than being out of doors. A disposable mask is not an option: it is *essential*. For the limited amount of spraying you shall be doing, something simple is quite adequate.

## OTHER THOUGHTS

There are some plastics however, from which paint will peel off for a pastime. It is the softer, soapier ones that offend most. Plastic curtain rail would be useful material for the garden railway modeller if it were not for the fact that it is usually brilliant white

and paint falls off it. Incidentally, I would recommend washing any plastic moulding in warm soapy water and leaving it to dry before painting. Mouldings may still have traces of release agent on them. On flat plastic surfaces, it may be worth destroying that perfection of finish by going over it with the very finest wet-and-dry paper. This produces those microscopic scratches that allow paint to bite on something and so remain there after long periods in the open air.

With experience, you find that you can use a whole variety of staining agents to get durable effects. The ranges of garden colours for woodwork have some interesting applications. For example, if you have cast a concrete base on which to put buildings or sculpted a rock face, the staining qualities of garden colours are very durable and long-lived. In the past I used to keep the dust I generated from turning iron castings on the lathe. This, when sprinkled over a natural rock face, gives a very realistic effect. Later on I refined this by 'rusting' plastic models by putting dilute glue on a model and then sprinkling iron flour over. When this is dry, a weak acid can be brushed over as an accelerator to start the natural rusting process. These days

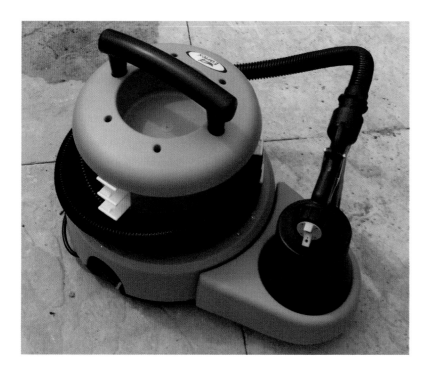

*A budget commercial spray unit has plenty of uses around a garden railway.*

it is possible to buy these elements in a kit from a model supplier.

What doesn't work out of doors is varnish: not unless you have a passion for rubbing down, sanding and repainting on a regular basis. It goes yellow, it cracks and it doesn't stop printed paper from fading. In short, over time, anything that forms a hard skin is to be viewed with grave suspicion. Buying hard polyurethane varnish merely means that the rubbing down is harder! So a general rule of thumb is that, where possible, use things that soak in. Model buildings can be painted with some sort of water-resistant clear liquid (Thompson's Water Seal for example) but, provided you have built them properly in the first place, it's ultraviolet light not damp that causes the real problems.

## SOME LIKE IT HOT

Live steam engines get hot. Some get very hot. Some get very *very* hot: so hot that ordinary paint blisters off. Those that are factory-made have heat-resistant finishes for obvious reasons. If we need to paint or repaint, the area of the boiler, particularly with externally fired engines, is the main problem. The answer is to use dull black barbecue (or wood stove) spray paint. Make sure the boiler is perfectly clean and dry. If it is made of brass or copper, it pays to put a coat of pre-etch paint on first, which gives the final paint something to grip on. The top coats of black spray will appear to dry very quickly but it is wise to put the model away for a couple of days somewhere dry before touching it again. If the dull black paint is too sombre for your taste, take a piece of smooth shiny cloth and gently rub the surface. It will buff up to a deeper sheen. Incidentally, this is true of most matt paints.

Strictly speaking, the boiler of a coloured locomotive should be painted in the main colour, not black. But in the cause of simplicity and durability, many people will accept this anomaly. Heat-resistant, coloured sprays are available – try a motorcycle store – but they can be sensitive to how well they are applied. I have seen quite a few failures over the years. If the loco is externally spirit fired, there is also a blackening of the outside of the boiler anyway, which is another reason to live with dull black. But if you really want to have a totally secure coloured finish then you need to look towards a company that offers high-temperature stove enamel finishes.

## BACKSCENES

If you have an unattractive block or brick wall somewhere in your garden, you may be tempted to paint a backscene on it. My first reaction would be to advise you to resist this urge, on the grounds that most backscenes I have seen detract rather than add to the railway. But if you are still enthusiastic then here are a few 'dos' and 'don'ts'. The first thing to do is to scrape off anything loose on top. If there is flaking whitewash, the easiest thing to do is to use a wire disc in an electric drill (make sure you are wearing a facemask and safety goggles). Prime the surface with dilute white glue or a proprietary sealant to stabilize things. Then give the wall a coat of pale-grey masonry paint. Just like lining a model, don't attempt anything you can only do badly. If you are hopeless at this sort of thing then paint some pale matt blue (all colours should be matt) at the top of your 'canvas', and then wash it down into a whiter blue as you go downwards, making the final brush strokes horizontal. Leave this skywash to dry. If you want to add clouds, splash some white paint up towards the top and then drag it sideways – try blowing it sideways with a hair dryer as well.

The usual mistake to make with the design of a landscape is to make it much too high. Try to really flatten everything down and stretch it out lengthways. Be satisfied with simple flowing shapes and leave perspective to the experts. Most of all though, use very gentle and light colours. There is such a thing as colour perspective. Distant hills are not Woolworth's Gloss Rural Green enamel. They are a hazy light grey/green. Tree trunks are *not* usually brown: they are a soft grey. A backscene should not draw attention to itself. If it does, it is not doing its job. Try painting a few backscenes with watercolours in a sketchpad first. It is quicker and easier to get the feel of it that way, before committing your first effort to a big wall. If you have some artistic ability then by all means make use of it. But don't turn it into a Sistine Chapel. The aim is to provide

*Painting a backscene: look at that simple, restrained colour. Notice too how flat and linear the landscape is. This also illustrates what we can mean by 'scale colour'.*

*The best way for a beginner to paint a realistic sky backscene on a garage wall is to think in terms of a variety of bluish greys, getting lighter as they go downwards. When in doubt, use less colour than you think you should.*

a fairly neutral setting for the railway to run in front of.

## A HEAD FOR FIGURES

Painting figures is a real art form. If you want to explore it, then by all means do so. Military modellers have taken the subject to new sunny uplands.

But I will suggest something simpler. In the large stage that is a garden, we may not seek to paint fine detail. Instead, what we are looking for is colour shape and texture. We don't see the whites of the eyes, even though we know they are there. A creamy-pink face has a darkened area around the eyes and the lips. There are slightly lighter areas along the nose and above the forehead. The underside of the nose is darker and the lips have just the

*Batch painting a group of figures. Restrained colours and a limited palette make things more realistic.*

*faintest* hint of orange-redness in them. A beard isn't gloss black and hair isn't shiny brown. Keep the colours gentle and work outwards from the face and hands. Apart from anything else, this is a quick method of painting figures, which can be unbelievably important when you have a lot to do.

To make figure painting easy, start with the face and hands, not worrying if you go over the adjacent clothing. Do the hair next and then the shirt and tie or blouse. The coat comes next, followed by trousers or skirts. You can already see that it is a case of working from the inside outwards. So straps of bags might follow. Shoes might be last. It makes a lot of sense to paint figures in batches. Keep all the colours restrained and matt. Visitors may not gasp in amazement at your painting skill, because your figures look so natural and real that they do not draw attention to themselves. They have a rightness about them.

Surprisingly, the one thing that is not a matt colour is coal! If you are painting those moulded plastic sheep droppings that some manufacturers insist on putting in tenders, paint them satin black – with a few small highlights of gloss. But it is far better to glue on some crushed-up real stuff anyway.

Painting is for protection and appearance. Keep ahead of the former and establish your own style for the latter. There is no secret to getting it right, just plenty of practice. When you start to build a garden railway, there are many processes that may be new to you. Painting models will probably be one of

*Even a cheap rubber figure will benefit from a paint job. Use an orange hue, rather than a red one, for lips and cheeks.*

them. The trick is in finding ways to hide your shortcomings until you become proficient. For instance, if you cannot quite paint a straight edge for now, do your best . . . and then draw a pencil line, with a ruler, over the edge, to hide any slight irregularities. It will look OK out of doors for now.

Painting is relaxing and therapeutic. I enjoy it, despite my own limitations. I would wish the same for you. It is something that people see in different ways. The converganists amongst us are good at doing very precise things: they make good model engineers. The diverganists are the arty folk. They will paint figures and backscenes well but will be hopeless at fine detail. Garden railways call for quite a broad range of painting skills. But don't panic. Like so much connected with the hobby, even if you have no particular skills when you start, you will find that you pick things up as you go along.

# CHAPTER 10

# Tools

Most of a garden railway can be built using ordinary DIY tools. I will assume that you have the usual essentials around the house and can use them, without necessarily being a craftsman cabinetmaker. If some of those tools are rusty, battered and worn then they should be laid to rest. Blunt tools are far more dangerous than sharp ones. It is customary for books of this nature to give lists of the tools you need to have, sometimes implying that you need to buy them all straightaway before beginning work.

*Just the right sort of small electric mixer for garden railways that use concrete.*

I will proceed on more realistic grounds. If you do need to buy anything though, try not to go for the cheapest in the shop. A couple of high quality chisels are much better than a big set of pewter ones. Cast alloy spanners are fine . . . until they let you down and snap. The worst culprits of all are cheap screwdrivers.

But let's strike off in a positive direction. I don't really need to say much about hammers (although it does help to rub a bit of emery paper over the face of the head from time to time). For delicate hammering work, life is much easier if you have a solid surface to work on. Ignore those twee little anvils. Instead, find a nice smooth chunky slab of metal. I have been using the base of an old clothes iron for years. Nearby I have a box of punches. One or two

of these are proper centre punches, but they are mixed in with all the odd-shaped bits of metal that have accumulated over the years to tackle punching jobs now long forgotten.

Marking out accurately on metal calls for a scriber. A new one won't break the bank but I got used to using the business ends of old darts. You can get a nice bit of tungsten steel in one of those. In the past it was usual to make your own marking fluid by mixing vegetable dye with shellac but, these days, a big felt marker does the job instantly. If something needs to be marked out on a big sheet of metal, I grab any old oddment of aerosol spray paint and give it a whiff or two of that. A steel ruler and a metal square are needed. Do remember that for awkward curved jobs, a sheet of paper is generally cut with true right angles. Indeed, all sorts of

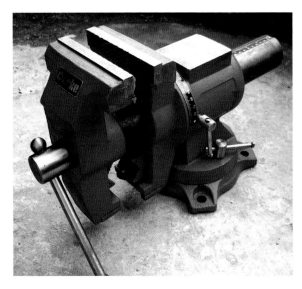

*A good sturdy vice is a big asset. If possible, try to arrange the installation height so that the forearm is horizontal when sawing.*

accurate marking out can be done with bits of wood, nails and string.

## DRILLING

A domestic electric drill is fine for major structural work and some modelling applications, particularly with a vertical drill stand to hold it, but for anything really accurate, a cheap bench drill of Far Eastern manufacture is a *big* asset. For general tasks it is far more useful than a miniature electric drill that comes complete with one hundred accessories. That can come later. There are some tools that look impressive on the workbench, but the first priority is to get the practical work done. Similarly, you may start out with a couple of drill sets in neat plastic cases, but you soon find that you use two or three sizes a great deal and the rest see little use. Make a note of those sizes that are kept busy and buy replacements separately. A sharp drill is a happy drill. A good rule, especially in thin material, is to avoid drilling a large hole in one drastic swoop. Use a small drill first and then increase the size in steps. Given a choice of speeds, always choose the slowest first and see how you get on.

As with all tools, don't let the march of technology blind you to the fact that traditional hand tools are often the best way forward. When I am drilling plastic sleepers, for pins to hold the track down, I use a small Archimedes drill because it is the most convenient tool for the job. If there is a chunk of timber to be sawn through, by the time you have got the circular saw out, plugged it in and then got the timber conveniently fixed, you could have sawn the job by hand and already be into your second cup of tea.

## CUTTING

The usual handsaws and hacksaws will attend to most of our cutting needs, but maybe there will be one or two new cutting jobs to tackle. If you haven't done it before, cutting a simple rectangle out of a piece of thin metal sheet can seem surprisingly difficult. I am not a lover of tinsnips myself and find that sharp kitchen scissors work nicely on very thin material. The trouble with thin material is that it is thin: thinner than the distance between the teeth of the saw. So angling the saw down flatter against the metal makes life easier. There is less chance of the teeth jamming against the edge because there are more in contact with the sheet at any one time. But even this may not be good enough. Sometimes it is better to mount the metal on a piece of scrap wood for extra support. This also makes holding the piece down on the edge of the workbench easier.

I can cut a fairly straight line with a hacksaw but not with a fretsaw with a metal cutting blade. If in doubt, I don't try. I saw as best as I can just outside the edge and then clamp a piece of straight metal behind it in the vice and file down to that. If you are coming new to cutting metal, it all seems desperately slow and laborious. You may despair about ever having the patience to do it. But it isn't that

*Amid the plethora of modern power tools available, simple is sometimes best. A small Archimedes drill is just right for drilling holes for pins on location.*

bad. You get into the swing of it. The secret is to use a sharp blade and let that do the work, not you. You can buy lubricants to make cutting steel easier but I use whatever oil is at hand.

Not having an expensive cabinet of modelling knives will not stop you from building a garden railway. A Stanley knife with a fresh blade can be used for most things. I find that it even tackles many delicate cutting jobs better than a modelling knife: there seems to be a bulk about it that gives better control. A scalpel from an art shop, and some spare blades, is just fine for delicate work in plastic card, card and balsa wood. In my workshop I have a large set of miniature wood chisels. I have used several of them on two occasions. Each year, I take them out of their box and lovingly rub some linseed oil on to the handles . . . and then put them back. Meanwhile the Stanley knife does the real work.

An electric jigsaw will find plenty of employment, including cutting thin metal. For doing decent jobs in thinner wood, use a metal-cutting blade for a cleaner finish. I used a bandsaw for many years and had no complaints. Eventually it simply wore out. I never did get round to replacing it so perhaps it was not as essential as I once thought. A hand-held circular saw is not a huge investment if your garden railway is going to include a lot of timberwork. But for most jobs, a sharp handsaw will do the job quicker than you would imagine. You notice how we keep coming

back to that word 'sharp'. It really is the key to an easy life.

A circular saw bench with a 10in (25cm) blade is a great toy to have for more advanced garden railway techniques such as baseboards with complicated geometry or making timber trestle bridges. I found that it is another of those tools that, if you have it, you will find all sorts of uses for it. But it is a luxury that can be managed without very easily. It is also a splendid device for creating mess. You haven't seen mess until you have used a saw bench. One advantage to using an electric belt sander is that it throws most of its dust into a little bag.

Sitting down with a catalogue of power tools is a dangerous thing. Take my advice and never do it. But if you must have power tools, do follow those safety rules out of doors. Protect your extension cable with a circuit-breaker and don't remove safety guards because they get in the way. If you must have a power tool, make a workshop vacuum cleaner your first one.

## . . . BUT PERHAPS NOT TURNING

Thus far, the word lathe has not passed my lips. For most things connected with garden railways, it doesn't need to. Even if you want to build a couple of live steam engines you can get by without. It is

*A low-priced laser spirit level also becomes a useful hand-held spirit level. I made an adapter for mine so that it could be used as a camera tripod.*

cheaper to buy in a couple of ready-machined components that to get a lathe. With machined kits now available, it is even possible to get into larger scale, passenger-hauling model-engineering type railways out of doors without one. I think I should introduce a touch of brutality here: new lathes don't come with a free voucher that entitles you to instant expertise in using them. If you have a particular yearning for the engineering side of things then by all means proceed. But it won't be the passport to an instant garden railway. Evening classes at college will help though.

A decent spirit level is a must. Because it is no longer a luxury item, I allowed myself a laser spirit level and this made me happy. But, again, it is not essential. A decent yard brush contributes far more to success than exotica. On the other hand, a budget bench grinder will pay for itself quite quickly in terms of not needing to buy new drills. An oilstone will give that final zing to a sharp edge. The sharpening of tools is a skill that is easy to learn from books. And, less obviously, if you are going to be doing a lot of digging, sharpen your spade first.

# SOLDERING

Without going into too much detail, let us browse through a few basics. You take two pieces of clean copper wire and apply molten solder to them with the tip of an electric iron to 'tin' them. Then you hold those two ends together and reapply heat, perhaps with an extra drop of solder. In a second or so, the solder cools and the two pieces are bonded together physically and electrically. You will encounter quite a lot of soldering jobs at this level so you might as well get a soldering iron straight away.

Thin wire solder will attach itself readily to bright shiny copper. But some jobs will call for a bit of chemical cleaning in the form of a flux. This is a paste that is painted on to metal and encourages the solder to bond. It is one of life's evil necessities, evil in that it is corrosive and therefore bad news for your skin. For general purpose small jobs it is common to use cored solder, which contains its own flux. Make it a rule that, whenever flux is used, you always scrub the job afterwards with a little domestic cleaning paste, using an old toothbrush. Otherwise the flux will start to eat into the metal and cause discoloration.

Homo sapiens has a design flaw. It has still not evolved the third hand required for holding two pieces of wire and a soldering iron at the same time. Until that happy day we shall have to get by with a cheap 'helping hands' gadget.

The soldering iron will be typically rated at 30W–40W. It will join wires and it will also attach small pieces of thin copper, brass, tinplate and nickel silver together. But as soon as a job becomes too meaty, heat is dispersed faster than our iron can put it in. So for more serious metalwork, we might have to treat ourselves to a big soldering iron: perhaps rated at 100W or more. Incidentally, don't let the ratings of 'instant heat' soldering guns fool you. They heat up very quickly but the tips are still quite puny.

There comes a point where it is much easier to use a small blowlamp on a job. Forget about those terrifying pump-me-up brass things; the modern gas-fired equivalent is much more of a precision tool. To use one, a hearth of some sort is needed. This is partly for safety and partly so that we can reflect large amounts of heat back on to the job. A little metal tray will do for small jobs. You need some refractory material that will absorb heat. Those flat bricks from the backs of fireplaces or line stoves are typical examples. Linings of cookers may well be useful. When you heat a job up on these bricks, the heat all comes back to the metal and adds to the power of the blowtorch. Thus even a small torch can solder big chunky bits of brass and copper together. We may be talking about very high temperatures but they are contained in a small area, so the volume of overall heat can be safely contained in a small area of the workshop. However, it still makes sense not to store paint thinners right next door to the hearth!

So far we have been talking about soft soldering. There are two further options. If we wanted to solder white-metal castings together, the iron would just melt them (skilled modellers can make use of this by fusing them together, but it is very easy to get this wrong and end up with fresh air and molten puddles), so you would use a low melting point solder and flux, together with a temperature-controlled iron. One common dodge is to plug a small iron into a domestic light-dimmer fitting. Low-temperature soldering is also useful if you are assembling many components close together. Joining part A to part B is easy enough, but when you try to solder part C on, part A falls off. So there may be an argument for using a low-temperature solder, and its own flux, on part C.

The other alternative to soft soldering is known as hard (silver) soldering. This is soldering with attitude! You need a bigger hearth and a bigger blowlamp. The flux, typically, is borax powder. The sticks of solder are expensive compared to soft solder. But it will solder a wider variety of materials, the joints are much tougher and can resist high temperatures. So you would want to use this for making live steam boilers. We are beginning to stray into model engineering here so I think that, having mentioned it (and perhaps brazing and welding as well), it can be considered as outside the scope of this book.

## BIGGER TOOLS

If you decide that your railway is going to be built with lots of stone or brick walls, concrete paths, decks and so on then a small electric concrete mixer is a tremendous time and effort saver. It also mixes much better than the average person can do by hand. There are plenty of makes to be had at modest prices. From a practical point of view, go for one that can sit on top of separate legs (the trick is to put the mixer face down on its barrel, stick the legs in the socket at the side, and then rock it upright). It is also easier to store, but make sure that the width of a mixer will go through an ordinary door (most do).

I think I will risk your scorn by even suggesting that there are good and bad wheelbarrows for use with garden railways. The most important feature is having an inflatable tyre. It makes pushing over uneven surfaces much easier. If you get a puncture, get a tube of 'green slime' from a bike shop and carry on with that inside. A painted box will rust quickly; it is better to go for a galvanized one. A builder's barrow is not always the best for our needs – it is heavy and can be difficult to move in tight

*This sort of wheelbarrow suits the less athletic garden-railway builder. Keep it stored upright in a dry place.*

areas. Having that 'U'-shaped piece of frame in front of the wheel makes tipping easier.

You will probably have the usual assortment of shovels, spades, forks and trowels around the place anyway. But don't begrudge replacing anything that has outlived its use.

So the moral of this story: you don't need to buy many tools to build a garden railway, but they need to be sharp. Enjoy the real pleasure of using good tools in good condition. Give any unpainted wood handles an occasional rub with linseed oil and spray a drop of WD-40 on metal bits.

## THE COMPUTER AS A TOOL

Useful things, computers. You can compile time-tables and stock lists. There's a whole world of reference out there about every aspect of garden railways, including societies to contact. But there is also the very useful facility of graphics manipulation. I am a Photoshop devotee and so my thoughts are based around that. But there are plenty of alternatives. Perhaps the simplest application is the type tool. We can lay out properly spaced lettering in all manner of fonts to use as templates for painting by hand. Getting just the right font can really set the tone and atmosphere for a railway. As well as whatever may be in the computer already, there are plenty of free downloads to be had, as well as CD-ROMs.

COMPTON DOWN RAILWAY

## PASS TO RIDE ON LOCOMOTIVE ENGINE

No.....................    Compton Down ....................*18* ......

*Issued to* ...........................................................................

*Available until* ....................................................................

.................................................. *Manager*

Before this Pass can be valid the Holder must have signed the Indemnity Book and had that fact recorded on the reverse, and also have signed the Declaration.

I understand that I ride entirely at my own risk and cannot hold the company reponsible for death or injury, howsoever caused. I will obey all lawful demands made by Officers and Servants of the Company.

*Signed* ............................................................

*Whimsical paperware is a good first experiment in making use of the computer as a tool. This lovely example was produced by Brian Spring.*

It is then a short step to creating miniature posters and enamel adverts by printing out directly. There is a problem that inks on printed paper are prone to fade and it's no good painting them over with varnish as this will make them go yellow as well! However, if you keep the file of the artwork handy, you can always reprint fairly quickly. Fade-resistant inks are available but don't expect too much longevity out of doors. But there are similar applications that receive less light. You can create a paper print of an ornately lettered side of a wagon or a van and paste it on to a plywood shell. Extra card strapping can be added and detail built up. Provided that the wagon is kept in a box when not

in use, it will look good for many years to come. You may also find that working with computer lettering will enhance your understanding of the principles of typography much quicker than by studying a book.

For those cold winter nights, there is a whole world of whimsical paperware to be enjoyed. You can create an entire railway in terms of tickets, notices to enginemen, special passes, posters for excursion trains: the list just goes on. Printing up a little Certificate of Visit to give to any visitors is a nice touch that costs next to nothing, except a bit of your time.

Aeromodellers enjoy the facility of sub-miniature cameras that link back to a small monitor TV or a

*Photographs of old or unusual signs can be cleaned up and resized in Photoshop or Paint Shop. Here are four examples. Feel free to copy them.*

PC. You can enjoy cab rides on your railway and share them with others via MPEGS and the Internet on your computer.

A useful feature of a good graphics program is the ability to start with a perspective photograph of, say, an enamel advert halfway up a wall, and then to be able to drag its corners in such a way as to render it into a truly flat, perspective-free image. A refinement of this is the facility to scan in a perspective photograph of a locomotive and to turn it into a side-elevation drawing. The Internet seems to be an endless source of drawings and images of all sorts of things, however obscure.

Here is an example of a specific project, aimed at competent users of Photoshop7 and later. It takes a photograph of a modern road sign and converts it to a model sign, specific to your layout. The first step is to convert the angled photograph into a flat subject. This is done by outlining an approximate crop and then drawing the perspective handles into the corners. If your program doesn't have this facility, try to take the photograph flat on, from a distance, with a telephoto lens. Thereafter the steps are as follows:

1. Adjust basic brightness contrast
2. Make the whites really white and the blacks really black (replace colour or levels)
3. Clone out any weathering marks
4. Magic wand any colour areas and accentuate
5. Clone out unwanted lettering
6. Save this 'blank canvas'
7. Enter new wording in appropriate font (the example simply uses Arial)
8. Save
9. Print on to glossy paper for a shiny/enamel finish.

*A modern road sign as photographed.*

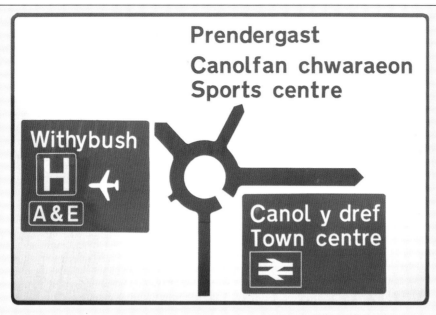

*It has now been squared up and the join lines/damage removed with the clone tool.*

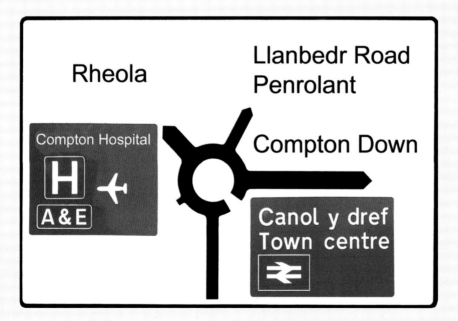

*The original wording is cloned out and then the whole thing has been cleaned up to reveal the basic colours. New wording suitable for the railway has been applied. If you want to try an experiment, copy this, clone out my wording and add your own.*

# CHAPTER 11

# Gardening

Although I cannot claim to be an expert gardener, with the passing years, little bits of useful experience have rubbed off. Some things worked; others did not. So perhaps we can run through a few ideas together.

One of the real benefits of building a garden railway is the introduction of hard edges between different parts of the garden. The edge of a lawn has a tendency to creep into adjacent flowerbeds, but a low brick wall slows it down. Even the very act of putting down neat boundaries tidies up a scruffy garden. I used to be notorious for my lawn. It was obsessively machined down to two thousandths of an inch and tended with loving care. I reasoned that this was the 'carpet in my railway room' and was kept neat accordingly. I didn't use ornamental grasses: they wouldn't have taken the heavy pounding. Instead I mowed the rough grass I found when I moved in, over and over, down the years. Repeated mowing of short grass with a rotary mower meant that I never had to pick the cut grass up and it always looked green. The lawn would stand up to wheelbarrows and much abuse. The expansion of my garden railway has now relegated it to history, but I was very satisfied that my régime was practical and the end result was what I wanted.

There are two ways of looking at planting in the garden. The first is to have a more or less normal garden, with the flowers one would normally expect to find. Through this setting, a railway runs. The lore and wisdom of gardening is well documented and you may go down familiar paths to happiness. The alternative is to use plants that are

*A neatly laid hard edge at work. A roll of split logs goes down into the ground and stops plant growth into the gravel. Under the gravel is a membrane to stop invasion from below, giving a tidy appearance that needs no maintenance. The end result is something that frames a ground-level railway nicely.*

*Further into the area, natural plants can run free. But you will notice a small piece of corrugated edging sticking up by the track on the left. It will stop the plant roots invading the track ballast.*

*Plants in keeping with the scale of the railway. They don't pretend to be models of real trees and plants but their size is harmonious. There is colour in this stylized landscape and everything hangs together well.*

small and in keeping with the scale of the railway. We are in a world of things with tiny leaves and low-growing habits. Mind-your-own-business may well carpet the ground realistically. Friends of mine have great success with it, as it quickly clothes everything with its greenery. Sadly, for some unknown reason, it just will not grow in my garden, despite many attempts over the years: one of those vagaries of nature. I particularly like filling little pockets in the rocks with suitably acidic soil and planting small heathers. Such things are hardy and look after themselves: my sort of gardening.

I think it is worth stressing that climates and soil types vary enormously. I live in a very mild part of the UK where frosts are rare. However, strong winds bring salt in off the Atlantic. So what works well for me may not be right for you. Instead of buying your greenery through the post, Internet or at a large garden centre, go to a small nursery in your area. Whatever does well there will suit the climate of your garden. You usually find that you can pick up good local knowledge there too. A friendly plantsman is a good ally in the cause of the garden railway. Try to avoid buying plants, for your specialist needs, from supermarkets or from garage forecourts just because they are cheap or convenient.

There is a large array of dwarf shrubs to be had. But do read the labels. Some pretty little trees can grow into pretty big trees. Again, don't go for

*The cladding powers of mind-your-own-business are amply demonstrated on Eric Lloyd's garden railway.*

*The ericas, including heathers, like a more acid soil. A garden railway can present a good opportunity for a suitable area.*

Perhaps you are not starting with a nice clean garden – you may well be taking over (as I did) an overgrown wilderness. In that case, it is time to roll your sleeves up. Hiring a powerful strimmer and a rotivator will save time and hard labour. This is no time to be timid – clear the site right down to a rough level and dispose of the newly uncovered rubbish. I didn't achieve instant perfection but I could see things much more clearly. It is often the best way.

something just because it is cheap. Go for what is right. After a while you can start to trim a few twigs from the base of these small shrubs and shape them into quite realistic trees. This is a relaxing occupation. I suppose that to go beyond this is to move into the world of bonsai, which may be a splendid hobby in its own right but not essential to our needs. However, it doesn't hurt to learn about propagation so that you can grow on from your own cuttings.

*Taxus is slow growing and adds a nice vertical element to the line of a garden.*

*This is not bonsai as such, but a dwarf bush can suggest a scale tree nicely. As you walk round the garden, snip little bits off bushes without really thinking about it.*

## PONDMANSHIP

I have to admit it: I'm now a pond man. There was a time when I wasn't. And now I am. I read up on it, joyfully thumbing through catalogues, and happily look after the goldfish. There isn't much to add

about integrating ponds into a garden railway and most of that is common sense. Bridges should have fencing to catch derailed trains. Try not to arrange things so that bits of railway can only be reached by leaning precariously out over the water. One friend discovered that solid fuel pellets for steam engines, accidentally dropped into the pond of a friend he was visiting, poisoned all the fish.

Having fish will alter the nature of a pond. It ceases to become a well-defined body of water with modelling potential. Instead it is a living habitat. As well as the plants you put in yourself, a whole subculture will evolve. This can be a rewarding hobby in its own right but it does demand your attention. I enjoy it, but not everybody does. Don't think of those live fish as some interesting accessory that you can simply add, like a toy boat. If you are worried about wildlife going after them, you don't have to endure the ugliness of a mesh across the pond.

A simple alternative is to make a plastic mesh that sits about an inch under the water level. I have used green plastic moulded fence mesh, stretched over a simple framework made of old plastic curtain rail. But a better alternative is to build up natural stone walls around the edge of the pond, so that it is just too far for cats and most birds to reach down. This also looks quite pleasing. If you think you may be troubled by such things as herons then planting a couple of vertical spiky things will interfere with their scope for flying in. Certainly, both still and running water adds to a garden considerably. As you may not want anything too ambitious, a strong moulded pond, properly bedded in, is best for a worry-free existence down the years. There are also many advantages to having flowing water. A submersible pump will push water up to a higher level (perhaps with a small filter box and a tiny pond) and it can then splash its merry way back from whence it came. This helps to oxygenate the water and thus keeps things fresher. But, of course, it also has a lovely relaxing sound to it. For that reason alone I have a personal preference for waterfalls rather than mini-fountains. But a typical small pump can be arranged to do either, just at the twist of a tube. With a bit of ingenuity you can also arrange for the pump to empty the pond for its annual clean-up.

*There is rich planting in this small, deep-set pond. It makes no pretence at being a model lake. The high surrounding area makes it safe to use as a nursery pond for small fish, free from the usual predators.*

*A mature pond, with a 0.16.5 scale railway being built. The strong framework of the bridge will later support more realistic detail. The moulded pond has a waterfall, which aerates the water as it circulates.*

## LARGER GREENERY

Larger shrubs can give shape and harmony to a garden. I might like my garden covered with railways but you may not. Tall, thin plants with light evergreen foliage seem to work best. Avoid the dreaded leylandii if at all possible. If you are unfortunate enough to have a neighbour who has planted it, there are two ways to go. You can be forever trimming the hedge neatly and carefully getting rid of every tiny clipping (they love to become entangled in track and line-side fittings). The more cunning way is to let the hedge really grow into your garden by a couple of feet. Then, use hedge loppers to cut right back hard to your boundary. This will take you well inside all greenery and it won't re-grow. You can then plant ivies. In a couple of years you will have a nice flat green wall that looks after itself and your neighbour will still have a hedge that looks fine on his side of the boundary. The other alternative with hedges is to deliberately shape them so that they look like a forest of individual trees on your side. It works particularly well with box hedges, but the ubiquitous privet will come up nicely too. It is surprising just how quickly it takes shape. Things should be looking reasonable within six to nine months. Moreover, the process is reversible. In a similar period of time you can be back to your flat green wall again.

Don't go for spiky things that will scratch you when they grow across the path. You might also like

*Larger bushes can form a useful backdrop to a railway. In this case, a rather stark fence is broken up. This is in the hard-to-define area of blending a small-scale model railway with a full-size garden setting. Descriptions are difficult but you know it when you see it.*

*A troublesome leylandii that is in the process of being cut right back inside its growth area so that it won't regrow lower down. Ivy could be used to hide the stark twigs.*

*Even in the dull days of winter, a box hedge, trimmed to look like a row of trees, has a satisfactory realism about it.*

*Larger greenery needs some thought to stop it swamping a railway with darkness. But, carefully done, it can provide dramatic effects. (Photo: Dave Lomas)*

to work out where winter shadows might be cast. But really, we are in the realms of everyday gardening here. For me the most important thing has always been the need to keep the maintenance as low as possible. I want to run trains, not spend time weeding.

*Simple traditional track, set in ballast, looks good on a wet day, when dwarf greenery runs along each side of it. A barrier is needed stop to encroachment, and keeps this timeless view just as it should be.*

*On the other hand, some plants might be considered just a little too invasive!*

## BACK TO NATURE

If you attend exhibitions of the 16mm Association and the G-Scale Society in particular, you may well encounter stalls selling plants aimed at garden railways. Here is really good treasure trove – for advice as well as for the plants themselves. However, if you have a yearning for a carpet of bluebells please don't take anything from the wild, raise them from seed or buy them 'ready made'.

An excellent school of thought suggests that merely having realistic looking greenery in the garden may somehow miss out on the splendours of the changing seasons. So, away from the track, you can allow yourself the sheer pleasure of watching snowdrops brighten the drab days. Running a train on a summer's evening will be enhanced if there is the sweet scent of honeysuckle in the background. And maybe, at the back of the garden, against a fence, you can permit some lupins or foxgloves to colourfully stand tall. You may not want to give yourself the work of putting in plants that flower only once. But there are plenty of things that can be stuck in the ground and forgotten about.

*The real delight of the natural look. A train can run through a setting like this that makes no pretence to be a model of anything: another example of the wide variety of ways in which it is possible to envisage a garden railway.*

*On a more practical note – a wildly overgrown privet hedge is chopped down, leaving some upright trunks in place. The clippings are interwoven to form a secure fence. It will regrow green in a year or two, or repeated sprays of weed killer on new leaves can kill it. But, whatever the choice, your privacy remains.*

## GOODIES AND BADDIES

Have a walk around your neighbourhood with a notebook. Check out what seems to do well in many gardens. Indeed, keep an eye out for things that do too well. In my area, fuchsia and montbretia can be rampant weeds: you will discover your own suspects. It makes sense to avoid things that are going to drop leaves and dead petals. Pine needles are a real nuisance – not only do they fall but they also lodge between sleepers. There are a couple of further things to note about trees. First, the roots of some species can undermine railway foundations and they can also suck moisture and nutrients from the soil around them. Apples falling from a height may not enhance your models. Leaves will fill railway cuttings, ponds and so on. However, if your garden has a fine tree or two in it, give thanks and live with the extra work. It is a small price to pay for such a blessing.

## NAUGHTY THINGS

It is possible that you may be troubled by a couple of really naughty things. Japanese knotweed is a ferocious nuisance in any garden. The proper thing to do is to dig out every last piece of root and destroy it. The only other option is to put down an impenetrable barrier and build a garden on top. If the site isn't too large you can get away with slashing the growth down regularly. I once had a garden that was half colonized by this menace but for some peculiar reason was completely free in the other half. The other nuisance, more newly come to gardens is Himalayan balsam, which is a pity because it is such an attractive plant. You can't go wrong with 'Mexican fuchsia' but they spread by exploding seeds everywhere. If you carelessly rip them out, you spread those seeds even faster. Fortunately the plants pull out very easily.

Couch grass provides an excellent fitness régime for anyone taking over a scruffy garden. It is major work to remove. Don't rely on the claims of many chemicals that say they kill grass. Couch grass drinks the stuff down, gives a merry laugh and then temporarily goes to sleep, lulling you into a false sense of security. If you have the time and patience, covering the area with old carpet, to exclude the light, for twelve months will do the job splendidly, but few of us can contemplate that. Putting down an impenetrable membrane and then building raised beds over that will work. There is nothing like a layer of concrete for bringing some sense of discipline to the beast. But, in the end, digging out every last bit may be best.

Unless you are addicted to serious gardening and hard work, the secret of getting things under

*Marty Cozad presents a view of a railway running through larger, more natural, surroundings. Everything is 'looser' than a more tightly manicured garden railway. (Photo: Marty Cozad)*

## GROUND COVER

*Ajuga is a practical ground cover plant. With its purple leaves and tiny blue flowers, it makes for an attractive general-purpose carpet.*

Because there are such wide variations of climate and soil types, I am reluctant to be too specific about plantings, but perhaps I can risk a few general notes about the sort of dwarf ground cover you might be considering. Perhaps the most useful family are the thymes. Get advice on particular varieties, but they are all hardy and adaptable – and also freely available at low prices. I particularly draw lemon creeping thyme to your attention. It is particularly hardy and nicely scented. Take a look at Veronicas and creeping junipers when you are at a nursery. Sedums and stonecrops are another popular group. Being succulents, they are good at retaining water so can do well in small pockets of soil that may dry out. But they are not suited to waterlogged soils. Alyssum is a traditional favourite of garden railway enthusiasts. For really large areas that need to be tamed, ajuga is a useful plant. It has purple leaves and nice little blue flowers. It is also a good weed suppressant. Ivy covers ground nicely – and eyesores as well. But it also covers anything it encounters if planted too close to the railway itself. Moreover, it will climb over any small barriers you may have put down in the soil. There are some lovely dwarf ivies that look much more in keeping with the scale of the model. However, be warned – some of these are so rampant that it is not a good idea to stand still next to them for too long!

## GROUND COVER *continued*

*The whole picture comes together nicely on Alan Craney's railway. The ground-cover plants contrast well with the neat roads and buildings.*

*Dwarf ivy covers areas of untidiness quickly. Care is needed as some can be invasive and creep through cracks into model buildings.*

*Wildness: seen through the window of my ruined abbey. I am happy to let weeds and nettles grow up around here. It helps the wildlife and seems in keeping somehow.*

control is not to try to get everything done at once. Each year, do a bit more to cut down on the maintenance and live with less than perfection for a while. In time your empire will become attractive and easy to care for. It will also blend in with what the family also asks of it. Having made a concrete base for a rotary clothes line four times now, in slightly different locations, I speak with feeling. The fact that it was my own fault does nothing to lessen my resentment at an unjust world. Places for children to play safely are more important than where your railway is situated. And remember: it's not the football's fault. You shouldn't have built that beautiful signal there. If there are children and other equally wild animals in the garden then it makes sense to keep things simple and rugged: safe in the knowledge that it should all get better one day.

## ALTERNATIVE GARDENS

We have spoken about traditional gardens. But there is a wider world out there populated with wood decking, gravel, paving slabs, stainless steel structures, abstract water features and so much more. A garden railway can be sympathetically integrated with all of this. The sweeping lines of a railway track can be bordered by natural greenery to

*Some garden details can be very simple. A neolithic burial chamber is made up of four pebbles and can be used to set off dwarf plants nicely.*

*Many of the elements of a well-balanced setting for a garden railway come together here on a wet day. The simple raised trackbed is supported on a pillar of stones, cemented together. A plant-topped pond merges into the scene. There is nothing complicated here but it works.*

form linear statements of something soft and natural that runs through a firmly structured garden. Indeed, it is possible to go further. The entire layout can be formalized beyond nature. Track beds can consist of purely functional timber structures that may be painted in a lilac-coloured timber stain. The focus of realism is thus directed purely at the trains themselves and their operation.

At the other end of the scale there is a garden that has a much wilder and more natural look (not to be confused with neglect!). The 'lawn' can be a meadow of wild grasses and the whole thrust of the garden is towards being ecologically friendly. Fallen tree branches make good habitats for all manner of beasties. The great temptation is to build the basics of a garden railway on top of this, in such a way that it will be overgrown and useless within a few months time. Being in tune with nature doesn't mean taking a break from common sense. The need for firm boundaries is even more important. You want to run trains, not do endless maintenance. So get the track up above ground level and follow the principles of foundations I spoke of in Chapter 3. Get those basics right first. Once this is done, there are various ways to harmonize your railway with these more natural surroundings. Clad the face of an elevated track with shrub or tree cuttings. Weave a rough fence with whippy bits, or nail up roughly chopped lengths of fallen/cut branches. Inside a year it will all have receded to the natural colours one would expect.

But let me conclude this section with at least one small tip. It will take several years for the garden surrounding your railway to start to mature into the sort of realism you may seek. For the first year or so, plant parsley. It looks like a fair representation of clumpy trees. Besides which, there aren't that many forms of railway modelling that you can eat!

# CHAPTER 12

# Operation

You might think it strange to read advice on how to play trains in the garden, but even here there are one or two useful ideas to consider. Being able to run a train at a moment's notice is a big advantage. So let's start off with a small box kept somewhere

convenient. It will have a modest battery loco in it and maybe a couple of wagons. The batteries should always in good order. As the magnate of a garden railway empire you may well have visitors who turn up unexpectedly, and it is nice to be able to show movement straight away. It also keeps their attention if you decide you are going to run something more ambitious. It can be trundling round whilst you are cleaning electrified track or raising steam on a locomotive.

You will need to go round and check for leaves, twigs and stones on the line. So keep a big paint-

brush in that cardboard box, ready to quickly flick things away. If the little battery loco does derail on something unexpected, *don't* try and shove it quickly back on the track with the wheels still churning round. It looks awful, it usually fails and it doesn't do your engine any good. Be patient – switch the motor off and check to see what the cause was. Put it back on the track and set it in motion once more. This applies even more to live steam locomotives. If anything goes wrong, for heaven's sake, *close the regulator.* Then sort it out.

Running a single train for your own pleasure is probably the sort of running you will do most. In truth, these are the occasions I like the best. But the next step is to run when there are visitors present. Your concentration will be divided. In the early stages you can make mistakes. But, after a while, you develop that sense of enginemanship. No matter what else is happening, subconsciously you are always with your trains, and will break off in mid-sentence in order to prevent some incident.

*A simple battery loco can be run at a moment's notice, even on the most unprepossessing day.*

*There are times when running a train is best done alone. On a foggy morning, enhanced by steam, you can enjoy the peaceful isolation.*

## HOSTING GROUPS

If you are so-minded, there are also opportunities to show your railway to other people. There are often small groups who are looking for interesting places to visit. They are invariably appreciative and they certainly won't nit-pick about an incorrect snifting valve on a smoke box. Groups of people with physical or mental handicaps are usually well supervised and when they have gone, you really do get a nice warm glow inside. If your audience is not made up of railway enthusiasts, then it makes sense to present your railway as a spectacle. Don't be embarrassed to slip a little loco on the track that is in the form of a motorized plastic rabbit. Keep the running simple and reliable, and develop the ability to talk interestingly whilst still keeping a discreet eye on events.

*Running an exquisite engine in the company of others needs particular care and common sense.*

You may very well conclude that ten is probably the maximum number of people your garden can cope with. You can also specify a start and finishing time. Usually a visit of two hours is quite sufficient. You will need to remember that you have a responsibility for the safety of your guests. Finally, it is their visit; don't be stuffy. Operate the railway and arrange things so that they get the maximum possible enjoyment, and you will discover that you do too.

As well as visitors who just watch, there will be those who come to run their own trains. I find that the best thing to do is to explain where the gradients are and any access hazards, then leave them to get on with it. Some people, however, are natural walking disaster areas. Give them a clear track and keep your own stock out of harm's way. But most will give no cause for concern and could well teach you a thing or two about train management.

Full-blown open days are big social affairs, very hectic and probably a bit chaotic. If needs be, put up a few guide tapes to keep visitors channelled in the right areas. You will need to offer guidance about where visitors can put their baggage, and park their cars. Some of the neatest modellers can be spectacularly untidy in both these departments. Open days are mentally draining but great fun. We are all different and so are our open days. To some it is an excuse for drinking and feasting, with some trains running in the background. Others are more concerned with the enjoyment of model railways. You will find some visitors just want to run their trains on your track and ignore everything and everyone else. Don't be daunted by this. Try to make their wish come true but also make it an opportunity to talk. Don't try and run trains yourself early on. You will be too busy chasing up a little spanner for someone, giving directions for the loo and just making things run smoothly – a temporary waste bin can be handy. You will have your own preference about whether to allow dogs in the garden or not.

Never judge the success of an open day purely by the number of people that turn up. On the contrary, an overcrowded event can be really quite stressful to all. However, it can make good sense to ask your neighbours if they would like to call by at some time in the afternoon so they can share in what is happening. After all, you have to live next door to them for the other 364 days of the year.

> There is a sub-culture of operation that is based on the purely functional raised circuit in the garden. There is a 'cult of the locomotive' to be enjoyed. The running of locomotives and their appreciation is the real attraction here. In some cases even a train of coaches is considered little more than something to bring out the best in an engine. For example, when you see a large Aster gauge 1 locomotive, it can be such a splendid object in its own right that people will forgather just for the pleasure of seeing it in motion. So what seems a worrying price tag at first sight, turns out to be the greater bulk of the expenditure and the final bill for a railway is similar to other formats.
>
> But because the models are just so exquisite, you will want to take particular care of them in operation – 'soft' fencing will prevent any derailments. On large sweeping circuits, speeds (and potential energy) may well be higher, and so rules of running more than one train at a time should be very much stricter. Besides, it is these locomotives that are the real stars. Smooth operation is the picture frame within which to show them off.

Of course, you may be someone who is not into social events. Your railway can be such a personal thing to you that you want to keep your privacy. If you find the garden a haven of peace and tranquillity, then by all means keep it that way.

## TIMETABLE OPERATION

Operation takes on a completely new dimension when we start to think about 'running a proper railway'. No longer is it just the pleasure of running trains. We will have constructed a timetable. Even a simple branch-line service, when run in the garden, can become quite demanding – a whole day can whiz by and you come off the end of your shift feeling tired! This is particularly true if you are using properly signalled block working, ensuring tail-lights and the like. Advanced forms of this call for more than one signal box to be in use, with proper communication. You are now running a railway. It is a stimulating occupation out of doors – particularly favoured by ex-railwaymen. I have even seen ad hoc block working suddenly organized with mobile phones.

## Compton Down Railway
### Winter Timetable 1887-88

| | | w | m | e | e | e | m | | e | A |
|---|---|---|---|---|---|---|---|---|---|---|
| Compton Down | d | 0600 | 0645 | 0900 | 1100 | 1415 | 1515 | | 1700 | 1830 |
| Compton | a | | 0700 | | | 1420 | 1520 | | 1720 | |
| Quarry Halt | a | 0615 | | | | | t | | | |
| Bedworthy | a | | 0710 | | . | | | | | |
| Penrolant | a | | 0720 | | | | | | | |
| Llanbedr Top | a | 0645 | | | | | | | | |
| Llanbedr Road | a | t | 0800 | 0920 | 1120 | 1435 | | | 1745 | 1900 |

| | | A | e | e | e | m | e | | m | e |
|---|---|---|---|---|---|---|---|---|---|---|
| Llanbedr Road | d | 0630 | 0805 | 1000 | 1200 | 1400 | 1630 | | 1700 | 1830 |
| Llanbedr Top | d | | | | | | | 1630 | | |
| Penrolant | a | 0640 | | | | 1405 | | | 1705 | |
| Bedworthy | a | 0650 | | | | 1415 | | 1640 | 1705 | |
| Quarry Halt | a | 0700 | | | | | | 1615* | | |
| Compton | a | | 0815 | 1015 | 1215 | 1420 | 1650 | | 1720 | |
| Compton Down | a | 0710 | 0820 | 1020 | 1220 | 1430 | 1700 | 1710 | 1725 | 1850 |

Footnotes
A – Motor train; limited accomodation    e – 1st class accomodation available    w – Workman's train; 3rd class only, Mon. - Fri. only
a – Arrives    m – Mixed train; conveys letters on payment of letter fee
d – Departs    t – Terminates above

CDR trains run Monday through Saturday except where indicated.
### NO SUNDAY SERVICE
Passengers are conveyed subject to CDR regulations, copies of which may be inspected at principle stations.    Signed, P.D. Jones  General Manager

*This 'recently discovered old timetable' (a Brian Spring masterpiece) was formulated to provide an interesting, but practical, operating session on my railway.*

With electrified tracks, there is also the possibility of another option for providing a spectacle. With advances in electronics, automatic and semi-automatic operation is quite affordable and much lower-tech than it used to be. Trains sweep around in all directions, lights flash and points change, while you sit back and enjoy the view. That view can be enhanced by any special effects you care to have. One simple device is to have a no-pressure boiler concealed in a concrete boiler house. A simple spirit burner will keep steam coming from a chimney and drifting over the landscape for an hour, without any attention from you. Loud sound effects are impressive but soon pall. I delight people with the proper change ringing from the tower of my model church for a few minutes – and then turn it firmly *off*! A waterfall into the pond is a soothing background sound for running a railway. It makes sense to keep it like that. If someone turns up with a commercial yodelling locomotive, let him or her enjoy a five-minute run before strangling them.

Turning things around the other way, perhaps you look upon your garden as a splendid place to indulge your hobby of building a model village, through which trains happen to run. Operation is simple and undemanding: allowing you plenty of freedom to enjoy your creation. And sometimes . . . nothing much need happen. You watch a short grubby train battle the torrential rain of a winter afternoon, preferably from a sheltered vantage point. It splashes through the puddles looking so much like the real thing. At the end of its journey, the loco will sit in its shed, dripping water as darkness comes. That has a magic all of its own too. You will be discovering your own niche in garden railway operation, and will get as much pleasure from it as anyone else.

For relaxed operation of a proper train service, perhaps the easiest system is to discard the notion of time entirely and have a sequential list of movements. You start with locomotives and stock in set positions and then, typically, the first movement may read: '001 = Lt engine from shed to siding three to collect empty coaching stock'. You can compile operating lists of varying complexity, including some that would allow you to languidly run a few trains on your own, but to a timetable. At

*Paths must be left for special services to be run. We can use our trains to carry tools to track repairs.*

*A tram-type vehicle makes for the simplest train unit to run to a timetable.*

the other end of the spectrum can be something that needs at least four operators to work.

An even simpler approach to relaxed running is to take a different view of realistic operation. This involves running the morning milk train before going off to work for the day. Or how about your railway doing a job of work? One example that immediately springs to mind is Brian Clarke's use of plum-harvesting wagons. We all dream our dreams in different ways.

## CONJURING TIMETABLES

Total timetable operation is something entirely different. It can derive from prototype timetabling or be a realistic application of correct railway practice to your layout. The simplest way to prepare a workable timetable is to draw the layout on a large sheet of paper and use different coloured matchsticks to represent locomotives and rolling stock. Have a starting position noted and then shuffle the matchsticks around, making notes as you go. Having established a viable sequence of moves, these can then be translated into a proper working timetable. If you particularly enjoy the challenge of railway operation, you can build in random factors. For example, a pack of 'playing cards', indicating freight that needs to be moved on a particular day, from which examples are drawn at random, can indicate which wagons will need to be used. This then determines what shunting problems you will need to sort out. This is best done by battery or two-rail locomotives. Shunting by live steam calls for a special kind of dedication that many people – myself included – just do not have.

Additional trains may be required. Thus when Compton Rovers play Dynamo Llanbedr Road, I would have to find the loco and coaches for a football special. Track maintenance trains, carrying small hammers, pliers and pins, may need to have track occupancy. Keen railway operators will also send out a breakdown train to deal with a derailment. The level of commitment is whatever you are comfortable with.

## SNOW

The first flurries of snow tend to send us into paroxysms of delight. Running live steam in snowy conditions is a rewarding assault on the senses. It looks good and has a realism all of its own. It is also cold! But we can live with that. The railway has

*All that thought you put into planning has now paid off when you actually run your trains. Even in a complicated scenic setting, easy access is maintained. That blank light area on the right was left as somewhere to stand safely in order to reach towards the back of the site.*

taken on a completely new appearance; it even sounds different. The experienced enthusiast will

already have built a big heavy snowplough to be propelled by a couple of powerful engines. But because of the scale effect, it can only tackle a couple of inches of fresh snow. Rather than spending lots of snow time trying to clear the track with a model, I cheat and go digging with a big trowel for a few minutes. Certainly, if you wake up to find the layout under

two feet of snow, don't be squeamish. Get the shovel going. When the track is clear and the trains are poised, take a few photographs. After half an hour of running, your fingers may be a bit cold for photography. Fresh snow is easy to run trains in, so make the most of it as soon as it arrives. Enjoy the moment. Whilst waiting for steam to rise, make a tiny model snowman and ignore the family sniggers. Later on it

*A fall of snow transforms this . . .*

*. . . into a completely different railway.*

*Following a recent snowfall, the sky is dark and ominous. But the trains are still running.*

'*We run trains to recapture something.*'

may freeze hard and running trains may be difficult. There is an even greater appeal that comes from running trains in the snow at night. If you do so by the light of a real oil lamp, the gap between your model and the real thing becomes insignificant. I'm sure there is some worrying psychology behind all this, but just forget it and enjoy.

Perhaps the common thread in all this is that we run trains to recapture something. We can be reliving our childhood or perhaps we are bringing huge working machinery down to size that we can manage and afford. We are modelling movement, often propelled by a bygone technology. We operate it how we wish, and take pleasure in the doing.

# CHAPTER 13

# Options

Most of this book is written through the medium of the commonly used G and 16mm scales because they represent the largest group within the hobby. But there now follows a brief overview of the many alternatives. As you will have gathered, the subject continues to be a dog's breakfast of ill-matched terms, with imperial and metric measurements in a wonderful muddle, which I shall attempt to unravel.

## SMALL-SCALE RAILWAYS

The minuscule Z gauge is perfectly feasible in the garden. The principles of two-rail electrification

*Many of the options available relate to scale.*

remain the same and so the minuteness of the scale is no barrier in itself. The quality of the track laying and cleanliness is paramount and so this is not the scale for running trains through loose earth at ground level. But then, loose earth is going to look massively over scale and crude anyway. Whilst all things are possible, I would suggest that you concentrate on running long electric worms over track that is laid on very flat foundations. All the natural enemies to garden railways are proportionally that much more threatening. I once had a seagull fly off with a tiny plastic coach in its beak. That might not have been so funny had it been a working locomotive.

You might well conclude that this very tiny scale misses the point of what garden railways have to offer in terms of space. But if this is your passion, then you can go ahead in complete confidence, although commercial support is limited. If you want something that has more of a modelling challenge, consider working to N scale but with a narrow-gauge feel, running on Z-gauge track and using Z-gauge mechanisms. A garden railway in a fat window box or even in an old sink used as a planter is quite an attractive idea if you are really stuck for space.

When you move up to N gauge, a vast range of commercial product opens its doors to you. You can buy most of what is needed for a rural GWR branch line, a Japanese metro or a long US freight train. Several diesel locomotives hauling fifty boxcars, as they snake through your dwarf canyons, are quite a sight (but make a re-railing device for putting those boxcars on the track in the first place!) Some commercial N gauge is, frankly, a bit crude when viewed closely indoors. But that becomes much less of a problem in broader garden vistas. Indeed, in all these smaller sizes, ultra fine-scale modelling may

*N gauge compared to 00.*

be rewarding to the serious modeller is livable but perhaps we can live with things being slightly more rugged. It gives durability and reliability: valuable attributes.

If you want to run narrow gauge trains on N gauge track then the trade is also very kind. 009 is the narrow gauge version of 00 gauge (4mm to the foot). There is good trade support, particularly in kit form. Closely allied with this is H09. This is the narrow gauge alternative to H0 scale (3.5mm to the foot), and there is considerable continental ready-to-run equipment available. Incidentally, it is worth mentioning that I am using simple terms to describe these narrow gauges. With US and continental railways in particular there are more elaborate codes.

For example, H0n2 describes a railway that is built to a scale of 3.5mm to the foot and modelling 2-foot gauge track in that scale. But let's not complicate things for now. A nice little challenge would be a 009 layout in an urn-shaped planter.

So that I am not accused of leaving anybody out, I will mention TT scale (3mm to the foot). Triang made a commercial system at one time and it still has its adherents today – many of which are excellent modellers in their own right and need no advice from me. There is also some continental product to be had. It is a minority sport but one which can be enjoyed out of doors.

So we come to the 4mm to the foot scale of 00 gauge and its chum next door H0, at 3.5mm to the

*N gauge compared with H09. You can see that they share the same track.*

*00 gauge is splendid out of doors. A weary Hornby 2-6-0 looks just right in the grey light of a winter's afternoon.*

foot. You can buy anything from a North Stafford-shire Railway buffer shank to a Pullman train without denting the wallet too much. Much of the trade uses durable plastic mouldings and reliable mechanisms. This is an excellent scale for those that hanker after running a busy mainline timetable with long trains sweeping over complicated layouts. The advent of digital control opened up a much wider field of operation. Being able to bring a train to a stop in a station and then fetch another loco out from a siding to double head it is rather a tempting concept. But even so, complexity is not mandatory. Not only does a simple branch line have its own rural charm, it is cheaper to build and easier to maintain. A line that wanders several hundred feet around a garden from station to station is a restful thing to watch in action. It is another way in which we can make good use of the space that a garden railway has to offer. Because of the rugged nature of much low-priced commercial 4mm equipment, it is possible to use the garden for complex layouts in this scale.

The 4mm scale can be considered as the smallest practical scale for live steam operation. There have been numerous examples of locomotives having been built to this size by competent engineers over the years but there have also been occasional

*We have spoken about the unlikely appeal of underground railways. A dark void is an intriguing way into a model railway.*

commercial products. The advent of the Hornby system has made small-scale real steam a practical proposition. I will suggest that this scale is also the smallest where battery power can be used in simple ways. A 4mm 12V locomotive can be powered by some AA batteries concealed in the coaches being hauled behind. It may well take some experimentation but it is possible. If the motor can be replaced by something running off 3V then life becomes much simpler. One useful tip is to use 'soft push' on/off switches to start the train. The kick from a conventional switch can be enough to derail a small locomotive.

For some years I have enjoyed running a small narrow gauge railway in 0.16.5 scale. This is to the conventional 0 scale of 7mm to the foot but running on 00 track, which is to 16.5mm gauge. There is satisfactory and reliable battery operation here that uses simple and reliable hardware. A rechargeable PP9 battery will allow a locomotive to haul a train along at a nice pace. This railway is really an extra indulgence I allow myself whilst waiting for paint to dry, or something, on my main garden railway, so I don't have as much time to devote to it as I would like. In a small concrete urban box of a back garden, one could build a very satisfying garden railway in this scale. There is commercial support in the form of many ready-to-run kits. But of particular interest is the fact that a cheap garden railway can be built using old 00-gauge track and loco chassis, with simple plastic card bodies and details put on top. This is just the right size for adapting things found in a rummage through the scrap box.

## MIDDLING SIZED RAILWAYS

Gardens were invented for 0 gauge. At 7mm to the foot scale, it has a bit of meat to it but is still manageable. In the USA, 0 gauge tends to be modelled to ¼in scale. Its use in the garden is a long and honourable one. Years ago there was a great deal of equipment available, often at budget prices. Sadly, it fell out of favour for a time, usurped by that upstart 00 gauge. But its return is greatly welcomed. We are mostly in a world of fine-scale modelling and two-rail pickup from the track. The

whole thing has a certain panache and there is a great deal of pleasure to be had from watching a train of lined out coaches gliding round the garden behind a matching locomotive. Scattered through this book are pictures of Phil Beckey's splendid railway. From these, you can get a feel for the way the size of this scale can be blended into a garden. You will note too that he has kept the track layout simple whilst showing how plenty of large curves sit nicely on the eye.

Budget ready-to-run equipment, such as is available in 00 gauge, is somewhat lacking in 7mm scale. The advent of Lima items heralded a brief revival and they got quite a few people started into the hobby. But supplies have been erratic and, in truth, our tastes and standards have risen.

Gauge 1 can be regarded as the meatier brother of 0 gauge. At 10mm to the foot you get a nice decent handful of model. There is a limited amount of budget product available as well as more exquisite hardware from the live-steam likes of Aster. To enjoy mainline operation in this scale calls for a larger garden. However, because the size is that much larger, the layout can be much simpler. A large circuit of track, perhaps with a station and a few facilities, will make for an impressive garden railway. The written word cannot easily convey the elegance of long trains under a summer sky.

Although mostly of US outline, there are cheaper commercial products to be had in 1:29 scale. These provide a good basis for making your own models in a non-engineering sort of way. As well as the 'express' end of the spectrum, gauge 1 is also nicely suited for use in building a rural branch line. Little tank engines haul short mixed trains as well in this scale as any other.

The 2½in gauge is another oldie. Its ancestry comes down through two routes. It was a model-engineering concept for hauling real people on sit-astride tracks. But it also had a format known from its old name of 'gauge 3' – which tended towards scenic model railways. You will not be surprised to learn that there are a couple of slightly differing scales to be found in the history books, but they can be ignored for practical purposes. Much more important is that, except to the pedants, gauge 3 is the standard gauge of which G scale is roughly the narrow gauge equivalent. So a gauge 3 main line

*The colourful magnificence of gauge 1 speaks for itself so well that just a functional circuit of track is sometimes all that is needed in the garden.*

could enjoy having a narrow gauge railway associated with it. In fact, we can take this a stage further.

However, gauge 3 is a bit underscale to dominate 16mm narrow gauge as it should. A better (if not perfect) effect comes from using the elderly model-engineering scale of $^{17}/_{32}$in to the foot, running on 2½in gauge track (I told you it was a muddle!).

However, I am delighted to say that a cause, long dear to my heart, is coming to life. Messrs Garden Railway Specialists are leading the way in producing affordable kits of small two-rail (or battery) locomotives and rolling stock. There is a satisfying mass to be had with these models but the technology remains simple. There are many temptations in this world that one can succumb to. Be warned: this is one of them. The sheer bulk of the engines and rolling stock gives a sort of majestic appearance. If you are undecided about the type of garden railway you might want, I strongly urge you to investigate seeing a G3 layout in action before you decide on an 'easier' scale that has more trade support.

## REALLY *REALLY* BIG

Although I have said that most things from 3½in gauge and above constitute model engineering, this isn't necessarily set in stone. If you like the idea of building a really big diesel-outline locomotive that uses the scrap box for its materials, then go ahead. Toy plastic pram wheels can have their tyres pushed off and one of the flanges carved away to make rudimentary driving wheels. The chassis can be made from plywood with a bit of metal tube for the

bearings. It can be driven by a windscreen-wiper motor, powered by a small car battery. Track can even be made out of hardwood rails to start with. It is just down to ingenuity. But a really big train, running through the garden, can be yours. At the more complicated end of the spectrum, small 3.5in gauge locomotives, built to full-blown model-engineering specifications, can be used to run a scenic railway, rather than hauling full-size people. If so, speaking from experience, I suggest that these engines do so at a comfortable operating height.

*Brunel's broad gauge is still to be seriously explored out of doors. This 16mm mock-up of a locomotive stands on 112mm-gauge track.*

*Very large-scale modelling does not have to be challenging. This large, whimsical locomotive was built out of plywood, scraps and an unknown electric motor/gearbox found at a jumble sale.*

## TRAMWAYS

This has been an area of modelling that has somehow been kept separate from railways. The trams themselves are the focus of the hobby. But out in the garden, there is a big overlap of building needs. So much of what has been written in these pages can translate into building tramways out of doors. This applies particularly to the smaller scales.

Trammery is available cheaply in G scale for those with modest ambitions. In the UK, rural tramway systems are scarce. However, the USA is home to many a system and they cry out to be modelled out of doors. The large 1.5in scale trams still tend to be the preserve of model engineers and craftsmen but, like all the other scales, there is a society devoted to the subject, wherein you can seek further guidance. But again, it doesn't have to be a technical subject. If you want to build a double-deck tram 6 feet long, out of plywood and the scrap box, do so. A windscreen-wiper motor and a car battery might drive it, but it will look imposing as it gracefully proceeds along its track, like a galleon in full sail. Trams offer the advantage of letting very sharp radius curves look realistic and they are shorter than a railway train.

## VINTAGE TRAINS

I like to see trains being run rather than kept in cases (or even in bank vaults). But for those of such inclination, it is quite possible to formulate a garden railway on which to enjoy the particular allure of vintage trains. The wheel profiles may be a bit crude and the track will have to match. Sadly,

*Municipal tramway modelling out of doors is a small but separate hobby – usually practised by craftsmen. But there is some overlap into garden railways. Bachmann G and 0.16.5 scale models of the same vehicle make for low-priced models in themselves or as resources for conversions.*

*Here a 0-scale, narrow gauge tram runs on 00-gauge track in a pleasant garden setting. In this case you have to imagine the overhead wire!*

*A steam tram outline loco is another area where trams and garden railways overlap. (Photo: courtesy* Die Gartenbahn)

tinplate sections of track tend to rust away out of doors. But to stay in keeping with the spirit of vintage railways, there are still white-metal chairs and chunky section brass rails to be had. These will run on over scale hardwood sleepers and it will all look rather splendid. It will all smell of creosote substitute, but it will be that empire upon which the sun never set. The engines may be clockwork or steam. If electric, they could be two rails or three. Stud contact is another alternative where current is picked up from studs with a long skate. Many of

the normal precepts of fine-scale garden railways go out the window here. We are creating the vintage feel of a traditional garden railway.

Vintage live steam can be, to put it mildly, exciting. At worst it can mean flaming balls of fire, hurtling down the track out of control. At best, they are old models that recreate a past age, still performing as they did when new. Out of doors, the budget pot-boilers tend to sulk in anything stronger than a breeze. But they can look imposing in motion and so we may forgive them their foibles.

Perhaps for the purist – and it is certainly good museum practice – the originality of the model is paramount. Replacing broken components with new is not acceptable and repainting is considered criminal. This falls outside the province of a book on practical garden railways. In our world, sympathetic restoration is perfectly acceptable. You could go further and re-engineer something totally worn out. New pistons are not obvious to the eye and fabricating a replacement for a missing burner makes sense. The next step would be to make more substantial new components – such as a cab or even a complete tender. There is an argument for turning a wrecked or broken model into a state that re-creates its appearance and performance when new, so that it can be enjoyed once again. You will make your own mind up.

By the way, if you think that conventional model railway scales are confusing, you should try vintage equipment. Up on my shelves I have locomotives of gauges as diverse as 2in and 3⅝in! We are surrounded by big, old open-frame electric motors, paxolin – and a crudeness that can be on a heroic scale at times. There have also been examples of trains that pick up *mains* electricity from live rails. I suggest that these really are best kept in display cabinets. But it all has a bygone presence that is hard to beat. Although you can enthuse over your trains as you run them, you will also want to look after them. So 'soft' fencing to prevent derailed trains plummeting to destruction is very worthwhile.

In this category too, perhaps I should include 'modern tinplate'. These are new models, in the spirit of vintage trains. There is a nicely nostalgic feel to them, without the worries generated by running old and valuable models. Some of them almost cross the border into being scale trains, but the tinplate ambience has a fascination all of its own, be it ancient or modern.

There is one more sub-group of garden railway enthusiasts: those who collect modern locomotives for the garden railway. This tends to be a somewhat expensive occupation, as might be imagined. The garden railway itself assumes less importance in the scheme of things. It is a setting through which to run examples of the collection. Although I do not aspire to these exalted ranks myself, I would suggest being somewhat careful about security to those who do. As with all forms of railway modelling in the garden, it makes good sense to photograph the railway and, in particular, your expensive locomotives. If the worst should happen, you have something tangible to show the police and insurance companies.

## WHIMSICAL MODELLING

One charming alternative is to indulge in whimsy and flights of fancy. The late Roland Emmet was the archetypal designer of the wondrously whimsical and designed his Oyster Creek railway for the Festival of Britain in 1951. You can follow his example today with tiny quaint engines, driven by similar figures. The art of the cartoon is to exaggerate existing features; so with your railway. Tiny engines with

impossibly tall chimneys can haul quaint carriages around sharp curves. They become almost like little creatures that scurry between their burrows. Indeed, they can be anything you care to make them. There are certain cartoon railway characters in books and on television which have faces on the front. By all means, you can adapt toys of these to amuse visiting children, but a really well-caricatured railway almost becomes a piece of art in its own right. They are also an expression of rebellion against taking life too seriously!

## AND THEN THE REST . . .

Thus far you have stayed fairly conventional. But the wider possibilities are bounded only by the scope of imagination. This may seem laughable but I model underground mine workings. When you

*A couple of whimsical little locomotives, as built by Graham Stowell.*

build stone or brick walls to raise the main railway up to a decent height, you can inset underground galleries into those walls. Apart from anything else, you can be making use of otherwise unused space without cluttering the overall appearance of the garden. The passing of the brass curtain rail has made monorails more difficult, but there are many variations on this theme. Rack railways need a reliable rack. There may be some question marks over commercially supplied racks and their durability out of doors. But it is a subject begging for further development. Cableways, Telfer tracks, cliff railways, pier railways: the possibilities are endless. How about a model of a miniature railway? If you have some spare N gauge equipment, convert it into a passenger-carrying miniature railway, using 16mm scale figures. A few tiny diecast model traction engines convert it into a model-engineering rally as well. If you are really stuck for space, Savages of King's Lynn once made a fairground ride that consisted of a tight circle of track around which ran a tiny steam engine hauling curved coaches. It ran through a canvas tunnel to cash in on the (then) temporary interest in a Channel tunnel. In Pembrokeshire

*The pole-road loco in its natural setting: something for the adventurous.*

*An old photo of a short experimental industrial monorail. Alas my interest developed some twenty years after the demise of the brass curtain rail.*

*Full-size railways of around 2ft (60cm) gauge can be extremely compact and will – surprisingly – fit into quite small gardens.*

*And here is proof: a complete 2ft (60cm) gauge railway in Brian Clarke's suburban garden.*

there is a narrow gauge railway system the sole purpose of which is to move full-size moving targets for tanks to shoot at (it does so from a safe location behind an earth bank!). On a military theme, there have been numerous systems that served extensive networks of caverns, which contained munitions. The permutations and possibilities are endless and it could be you that may broaden the scope of this hobby in your turn.

As for the rest of the rest – a lot of it could be US practice but there is so much else still waiting to be modelled in the garden. Railways that ran in the Australian outback, Austrian steelworks, Japanese backwaters and South American pampas . . . the list is enormous. After cutting your teeth on ready-to-run hardware to get the feel of things, you can broaden the scope of garden railways with your own pioneering. And I thank you in anticipation.

*An obsession becomes a reality. Here is my non-working replica of a Kerr Stuart Wren.*

# CHAPTER 14

# Passenger-Carrying Railways

*A large narrow gauge tank engine offers a roomy cab and easy access to simple controls.*

Let me shift the emphasis now, away from model railways as such, towards small railways that haul real people. These are generally referred to as miniature railways, rather than models. It is possible to build a circuit of track in a garden that is only 15ft (4.5m) wide. Alternatively, one can get simple pleasures from a straight run of perhaps 40ft (12m). Final costs are not high and there is a unique pleasure in running what is, after all, a real railway. Rail section is available in all scales. Complete kits of track panels may typically consist of

steel or aluminium rail, wood sleepers drilled to gauge for fixing screws and the fixings themselves, together with suitable rail joiners.

In the early days of the hobby, tracks were mostly raised above ground level and the passengers sat astride the trolleys, for stability. This is still much favoured by tracks belonging to model-engineering groups. It does mean that 2½in gauge is viable for passenger hauling. The attraction of this scale to model engineers was that live steam locomotives could be built on the modest-sized, sometimes treadle-powered, lathes of the past. People would almost be overawed by the sheer bulk of 3½in gauge models. With the advent of affordable larger machine tools for domestic use, 5in gauge has become commonplace. For ease of driving and the stability of passengers, functional above ground track has much to commend it.

## BUILDING ELEVATED TRACK

There are many ways of building the foundations for such a track. The simplest would be to build a low single wall of concrete blocks on a concrete foundation. The height above ground level would typically be that of the seat of an ordinary chair. So two blocks, on edge, high (18in/450mm) would be about right. The track would be plugged into the top of the blocks. The result will be maintenance free although not very attractive. A nicer addition to the garden would be to build a double brick wall with an interlocking bond. There is obvious scope for decorative brickwork with arches or piercings, if such things appeal. Both block and brick construction give scope for sinuous, curvy meandering around the garden. This usually looks more harmonious than geometric straight lines and curves.

The next alternative is to use piers and beams. The piers could be of simple brick construction with cast concrete beams stretching between them. Ideally there needs to be some means of holding the beams in place but allowing for adjustment up and down. So you would be looking at having short projecting steel rods on the piers. Holes cast in the beams would locate over these and rest on packing (rubber padding is particularly sympathetic). Be warned though: a well-cast concrete beam is taking us into a world that is fraught with heaviness. Lifting such things is not a one-man job.

An alternative is to use a light steel construction for those beams. Pairs of old bedframe angles, bolted together with spacers, make excellent foundations for a garden line. It is worth asking in scrapyards or at furniture reclamation centres for such things. One particularly useful material used to be old point-rodding that was made redundant when British Rail closed lines that had mechanical point operation. However, this golden era seems to have passed now. For an easier life, timber beams can give good service. Buy pressure-treated sawn timber. Typically a piece of 4 × 2in (10 × 5cm) timber will be edged either side with 6 × 1in (15 × 2.5cm) on edge, thus forming a girder. The beams will be straight, of course. Your track will probably want to curve. So the beams are made shorter and set at angles and the track is allowed to curve on top of them. This works well for large-radius curves but for anything sharp it is back to the bricks or blocks.

*In this case, steel rail section is screwed to sleepers made from strips of reconstituted plastic.*

*Functional elevated track, built using concrete blocks and old point rodding.*

You will have immediately realized that, with a sit-astride track, points are not an option. If you want to 'break into' the track, you will need to build a section that slides sideways on runners (a traverser). If you visit club layouts around the country, you will find all sorts of variations of these. Five-inch gauge steam locomotives are *very* heavy things. Steam will be raised in a steaming bay and then the loco is transferred to the running track. With a small garden line you may well feel that you don't need to go this far. This doesn't have to be the province of live steam. A simple battery loco, which hauls a couple of people, is manageable for weight and doesn't involve the big step of moving into the challenging world of coal-fired live steam.

*A waist-level steaming bay is invaluable for preparation and disposal of locomotives. In this picture it is acting as a stand for a fibreglass body shell of a battery locomotive.*

## GROUND-LEVEL TRACK

It is when you move down to ground level that the feeling of 'real railways' begins. You excavate the trackbed, put down a weed-resistant membrane (such as roofing felt) and put a layer of rubble in the bottom for good drainage. Order a few tons of chippings, the suitable size of which will vary depending on the scale you are working in. But avoid the temptation of buying 'three-quarters to dust' because it may be cheaper. That dust will bind nicely but it will provide a fruitful home for weeds later on. Tip the chippings into the trench and consolidate by trampling on it. The track is laid and then ballasted neatly. This really is a most enjoyable task.

With track laying on this scale there is a strong aesthetic bond with the real thing. There are several reasons for ballasting. First, it provides a resilient base to make the track more comfortable to ride on. Second, it provides a gentle grip on the track, which is easily adjusted. If part of a length of track has a dip in it, then shovelling a little extra ballast underneath can build it up to level again. Finally, and perhaps most importantly, it keeps the wooden sleepers away from lying water. Try to avoid having earth or plant life invade the ballast as this interferes with free drainage.

Because you are building a 'real' railway, rather than a model, the track will be functional, rather than fine-scale. For 5in gauge, a sleeper might be a 9in (23cm) length of 2×1in (5×2.5cm) sawn timber, spaced at 2½in (6cm) from its neighbour. I

*Ground-level 5in gauge track in a small garden. If you walk on your trackbed a lot, try to avoid using the unsupported aluminium sleepers sometimes available in track kits: they buckle under careless feet. Add wood reinforcement underneath or use wooden sleepers instead.*

*If you have space, don't be afraid to work the track up into something with more ambitious civil engineering.*

## FINAL BALLASTING

With the track sitting fairly flat on well-trampled ballast (if you can borrow a small vibrating roller, so much the better), loose ballast is tipped generously and spread out with a yard brush and shovel. Take some time to really level the track accurately by eye. There are devices to aid this but a spirit level and your bottom on a rolling wagon is as good as anything. Tamp the ballast down so that it fits neatly between the sleepers. Be prepared for the track to 'move' a little during the first weeks, until the ballast has really consolidated. It also likes to dip at rail joints, unless well supported.

*A neat simple track! In this case it is 7¼in gauge and a pleasing sight in its own right.*

again express a personal preference for using pressure-treated softwood, rather than a hardwood. It seems to absorb subsequent coats of preservative better. I have sleepers that have been out of doors for more than thirty years now and are still in good condition. However, you will find alternative opinions. I particularly commend the practice of using reconstituted plastic for sleepers. You will probably have seen this material in use for park benches, but it can be bought in strips and sections. It is weatherproof and it also gives a smoother and quieter ride. A piece of metal is drilled out to form a drilling jig for pilot holes in the sleepers. Into these go panhead or hex-head screws to hold the rails in place to gauge. It is quite common to have dual-gauge or multigauge track.

For home use, aluminium rails are fine but could wear quickly under heavy club use. Steel rails are more durable. Whichever are used, wood or plastic sleepers add further to the resilience and comfort of the ride. Having steel rails welded to steel sleepers, and pinned directly to a concrete base, is not my idea of comfort. It is possible to economize by using ordinary steel bar as rails, but the sharp corners are not kind to wheels over a long period of time. Besides, having proper rail-shaped rails adds to the rightness of it all in a garden setting. Rail ends are not fitted rigidly together. They are clamped together by fishplates (rail joiners) that allow for a little expansion and contraction in different temperatures.

As with model railways in the garden, if sharp curves are needed, it pays to pre-bend the rail. When faced with bending rails for a 5in gauge track, I cobbled together a rail-bending service with bits of bedframe and some old skateboard wheels.

Down at ground level, points are possible and this greatly simplifies things. Sit-on passenger trolleys will run on 3½in gauge track but this is a precarious practice. Five-inch gauge gives more stability and is the smallest gauge in common use. A passenger vehicle might consist of a welded or bolted steel frame, to which axle boxes have been added. These can be made of a metal bearing or ballraces. Simple disc wheels suffice. They will be overscale thickness and fitted to chunky axles. The easiest coupling is hook and chain, but it is better to have a solid bar link between the locomotive and front trolley. This prevents 'shuttling' and banging. It also avoids the need for buffers on the passenger vehicle. The wise enthusiast will make the trolley as comfortable as possible with a low seat topped with a soft cushion. I was brought up to believe that any fool could be uncomfortable!

## BATTERY LOCOMOTIVES

Simple locomotion can be typically provided by a bolt-together kit for a diesel-outline engine that runs off something like a car battery. It will only take a few days to assemble with hand tools and paint. The body will be either a metal casting or a fibreglass moulding; the controls will consist of a forward-neutral-reverse switch, perhaps with the option of an electronic speed control circuit. There could be some lights and maybe a little horn. It will be easy and safe to drive, and maintenance will be minimal. If you are feeling ingenious you might even feel like building an alternative body in ply-wood and aluminium. Such a compact loco will look right hauling a couple of short passenger trol-leys in a small, sharply curved layout.

There are further levels of refinement if you are feeling more ambitious. Bogie diesel-outline mod-els are available, which offer more power. There are also kits of steam-outline models. A study of the model-engineering press will lead you to these. Some manufacturers also offer the option of power

by a small internal combustion engine. In a mod-est-sized garden, surrounded by neighbours, I would be inclined towards the quietness of battery power (and enjoy the no-fuss operation).

*More ambitious is this battery-powered 5in gauge Bulleid Pacific. The body moulding really does capture the feel of the real thing.*

*Moving further up in size, we see a narrow gauge diesel loco running on 7¼in gauge track. We are starting to get into the realms of serious passenger hauling here.*

*There are plenty of simple kits available that bolt together very quickly. This is a large model with a narrow gauge outline. The power comes from a small 4-stroke engine but battery power would be a common option.*

*Eventually things reach a stage where passengers can sit in the coaches rather than on them.*

## THE ULTIMATE EXPERIENCE

The ultimate driving experience comes from coal-fired live steam. But you have to accept that to enjoy this, you will be moving up to a completely new level of complexity. Building one in the traditional way calls for a well-equipped workshop and knowing how to use it. Even then, you need to be prepared to spend a couple of years working solely on this project. If your interest is primarily aimed at a garden railway, you could well conclude that it is more practical to buy a second-hand loco in good working order. There are dealers in such things and there are the small ads in magazines. If you are a complete beginner, be very wary of buying a part-built model. Even if there is only 10 per cent left to do, the work entailed could be well beyond your capability and equipment. There is also the danger of the blind alley. Someone will have made a good start on a model and it may look all very nice. But it is likely to be for sale because there is some fundamental flaw which means that building cannot continue without going right back to the beginning and re-designing some major component. So don't get carried away by the bulk of all that shiny metal in front of you.

An alternative is to buy a machined kit in stages. This may seem expensive but that just reflects the sheer complexity of live steam. These aren't models; these are full-blown steam railway engines that are small. The makers of these kits usually claim that they can be assembled merely using hand tools. This may be true, but not in all cases. There have been examples of bolt-together kits that needed further engineering to get them to work. The best thing is to visit a model-engineering society or ask around. Their grapevine is usually in excellent working order. They will be a valuable repository of practical advice anyway, and will welcome the sniff of any new blood to their ranks. The chance to see various locomotives running may give you a better idea of what it is that you really want. A simple, chunky narrow gauge tank engine is often easier and more comfortable to drive than a fine-scale express locomotive.

I hope that you will not be put off by this litany of warnings. Driving a big coal-fired loco is a magnificent way to spend one's leisure time. Indeed, it is a hobby in its own right and the trappings of a garden railway can seem less important, if such is your inclination. It feels right, it smells right and

*A little 3½in gauge loco will trundle happily up and down a small garden, pulling one or two adults. A small engine might be a challenge for a beginner to drive on a long club track, but it can be built on a modest-sized lathe.*

there is real satisfaction to be had from good enginemanship.

## AMBITIOUS CIVIL ENGINEERING

A passenger-carrying railway – particularly a ground level one – can be treated as a large garden railway, with all the trappings and fittings that go with it. A waiting room can be the same shape as the other railway buildings. A small signal box can control signals. The line can cross a pond with a small bridge. There can be turntables, level crossings, signs, and small lights. The list is endless. If you have room, don't be afraid to rearrange your ground so as to incorporate a tunnel or an overbridge. If you want to get carried away with civil

engineering then by all means do so. But do remember that good principles of structural engineering still apply – even in miniature. So don't be tempted to over-reach the extent of your knowledge. In short, a complete railway can be created in the garden. You will sit behind the engine but there is nothing to stop you from hauling a train of model wagons or coaches behind you.

## SMALL REAL RAILWAYS

There is one last step you could take although it stretches the term 'garden railway' to its limits. It is possible to build a full-size narrow gauge railway in a reasonably sized garden surrounding a semi-detached house. Two-foot gauge light track can be laid from front to back, possibly with rails inset into

*The author's 5in gauge tank engine was a good chunky beast that would fit into the boot of a car. Alas, as the years advanced, it became too heavy, and has now been sold out of service.*

*Surprisingly, once a loco gets over a certain size, weight becomes less of a problem. Things reach a stage where trailers and winches are needed. For the driver it now becomes more a case of sitting in, rather than behind the engine. But be advised that, as you might expect, we are into the serious money here for something ready to run.*

the drive if it crosses it. The curves of light industrial track can be remarkably sharp because the trains were often intended to run in very confined spaces. Thus the hardware can be very bijou indeed. There is room for sidings, little engine sheds and whatever else takes your fancy. Actually, this isn't as radical as it sounds. A small diesel loco might have a footprint of roughly $4\frac{1}{2} \times 7$ft (roughly $1.5 \times 2$m). A couple of tipper wagons will form a short train and joy is unconfined. The locomotive will sound like an old concrete mixer and issue diesel exhaust. So some consideration for neighbours is in order.

But there are simpler alternatives. A tipper (skip) chassis can make the basis of a simple locomotive given some sort of low-voltage traction motor and a lorry battery. The butchery will probably involve a motorcycle gearbox and chains, but it can all be hidden under a quaint tram engine body. Unless done with superb taste, there is no way that the resulting railway is going to make the front cover of a gardening magazine. But if you want it, do it and enjoy it.

Passenger-carrying railways call for a lump of money to be spent on a locomotive early on. By the time the railway is complete, you will have filled your garden with something that probably cost about the same as doing so with one of the garden gauges. I suggest that the appeal of passenger hauling is more narrowly based than the broader picture of running a garden railway. But it is there for the taking if you want it. I have 'put down a bit of five inch' to supplement the 16mm garden railway and so, like others who have done so, get the best of both worlds.

## DRIVING THE BEAST

So let us get a feel for what running something larger is all about. Your steed will be a 5in gauge 0-4-0 tank engine. The first thing you notice is the sheer imposing mass of it. It is *big* – to the extent that it is more like sharing its presence than looking at a model. Big bits of machined bright metal sit there in an imposing way. Because it is a fully functioning machine, it looks rather complicated and daunting at first glance. The fact that it needs a boiler certificate gives

us pause for thought. This is a serious railway engine. Fortunately, like anything else, it all becomes familiar with practice and loses its mystery – especially if you are guided through your first few drives by someone with experience.

So, put it on the track. Good grief – heavy, isn't it! It is really a two-man lift for comfort. As its weight goes on to the rails, it sits down on its springs nicely. The handbrake is screwed on and you check the water level in the boiler, using the gauge glass on the boiler backhead. If it is a bit low, you can use a built-in hand pump to transfer water from the tanks to the boiler until the gauge shows about three-quarters full. You then make sure that the tanks are filled up, using a hosepipe.

*Just in case you think that driving a steam engine would be too difficult for you, be* very *ashamed. The safety goggles are a good idea.*

From your box of steaming-up bits you take out a jar of wood chips that are soaking in paraffin. Some of these are popped through the fire hole door, on to the grate. Now for something odd: you also fish out a small, all-metal electric fan sort of gadget and stick it over the chimney. Because the difference in height between fire and chimney is only a few inches in our model, you don't get a natural draught. So you use this little 12V auxiliary blower (well, it's a sucker really). This is switched on as you apply a flame to those wood chips and they burn up straight away. Quickly add a few more and then switch over to using dry chips. This reduces the blue oily smoke coming from the chimney. The dry chips crackle merrily in the grate. Very slowly, start adding either small lumps of steam coal or anthracite. Household coal smells lovely but tars the inside of the boiler.

Experience tells you how quickly to add the coal, but that auxiliary blower keeps things burning nicely. Whilst keeping an eye on the fire, fill up the lubricator with proper steam oil, and then oil round the moving parts, checking to see that all is in order as we do so. Soon, the little column of water in the glass is starting to bob up and down: a precursor to the needle of the pressure gauge starting to move. Once there is 'twenty pounds on the clock' the blower valve is opened. This lets a fast thin jet of steam shoot up the chimney, sucking your fire with it. So you can thankfully remove the auxiliary blower, and its irritating buzzing noise, and enjoy the sound of steam. But still you need to keep topping up the fire, a few lumps at a time. To run a steam engine, a pleasantly burning fire is no use. What you need is a bright red-hot bed of coal generating a great deal of heat. That forced draught is needed to create this.

*If you are of an original turn of mind and want to try out new things, here are a couple of suggestions. First, a tiny 3½in loco that is purely for scenic use, (although it would look attractive as a passenger hauler in a large scale). It could be battery-powered or run off a geared oscillating cylinder hidden away somewhere. As I recall, the wheels were made from old clothesline pulleys with one flange turned off!*

*Here we see a simple experiment to consider a 5in gauge coal-fired loco as a scenic engine, hauling wagons and coaches, at waist level. It would have been fairly simple to fit radio control but I never did get round to it. Perhaps someone else might take up this particular torch.*

With pressure approaching the blowing off point, when the safety valves lift, things get busy. Bring up the driving trolley and couple it up *very securely*! Raising steam has consumed water so you need to top the boiler up. A loco injector is a marvellous bit of kit. There are no moving parts and so relies on a combination of cones to incorporate steam from the boiler with water in such a way as to increase the force enough for that water to be injected into the boiler, against the boiler pressure. Turn on the water first, and a trickle runs down on to the track. But when you open a steam valve, the

trickle stops and there is a lovely singing sound that tells you that the injector has 'picked up'. You won't want to suddenly put a lot of cold water into the boiler because that would knock the pressure down. Instead, do it gradually. What you are aiming for is a good water level, a deep incandescent fire and the safety valves just starting to lift.

When this happy state has arrived, use your eyes to make sure that it is safe to do so first. Because passenger hauling has moved you up to a whole new level of mass and energy, drive with care, even if just running up and back along a little stretch of track in the garden. But, satisfied that all is in order, open the cylinder drain cocks, put the engine in full forward gear . . . and gently open the throttle. If this is your first time, it is a seriously nervous moment.

## MOVEMENT AT LAST

To your surprise, the train moves off, hauling us like a bag of feathers. Fighting back the urge to panic, there are various things to be done. The most important of these is to keep your eyes on the track ahead of you. An experimental close of the regulator will slow the engine down quickly. Now that you know how to stop, re-open it and gather speed again. A feeling for the inertia and rollability of a train soon comes – including the difference that slight uphill and downhill grades make.

After a short distance, the cylinder drain cocks can be closed. If the track is an end-to-end one, when you reach the far end, stop in good time. Once stopped, check the water level and the state of the fire. If the boiler is blowing off then adding a dash of cold water to it with the injector will calm things down. For your first drives, it is better to make adjustments when you are stopped, if possible, until they all become automatic. When the train is chuffing along merrily, the blower valve can be closed, but you must remember to open it every time you stop. This soon becomes as automatic as breathing.

Keep on firing, little and often. The aim is to maintain a reasonable bed of very bright red fire. Be fussy about always keeping the firebox door closed unless you are actually putting a shovelful of coal in. The art of driving is mostly centred on keeping a good boiler pressure balanced with a nearly full boiler. The new driver has to think about all these things and, if possible, it helps to have someone behind him with a few reminders. But as everything starts to gel then it is time to move on to more refined driving.

The exhaust will be barking away when the train is on the move. Particularly on a continuous circuit, once you have got things settled, think about cutting off some of the steam from the reversing lever. By moving it back a notch, a smaller amount of steam goes into the cylinders with each stroke. The 'bark' becomes quieter and you are using less steam. When you come to a stop you will close the regulator and put the lever in 'mid-gear' (not forgetting to put the handbrake on). When you start again, you will put the engine in full forward gear before opening the throttle (or full backward if you want to reverse).

With so much to think of, time soon passes. It might be as well to check the lubricator to see how the oil level is doing. Run the poker through the fire just to rake down any ash. You are slowly becoming an engine driver.

## WINDING DOWN

And that good driver is always thinking ahead. Knowing that the end of the run is coming, the fire can be left to burn down thinner. As the engine stops for the last time, the injector is knocked on to top the boiler up for another day – and also to reduce any excess steam. Don't forget the handbrake. The remains of the fire are raked vigorously through into the ash pan. There will probably be a dump pin on this. Pull it out, and the hot ashes fall down on to the ground below. Sprinkle them with water for safety. Put the blower valve on gently to allow any remaining pressure to slowly escape.

Meanwhile, go round to the front end and cover the front buffer beam with an old rag. The smoke box door is opened to reveal a surprising amount of ash. This has to be shovelled out and the surplus brushed away. Next job is to put a proper flue-brush through the tubes to clean them. Brush away any rubbish from the front and close the smoke box door again, making sure no grit is trapped. This door needs to have an airtight seal.

By now the fire bars in the firebox should have cooled down. They may well need to be removed for cleaning, but certainly they will need to be brushed absolutely clean. The ash pan is replaced and the entire loco is given a clean whilst it is still warm. A mixture of paraffin and engine oil works well. When everything is spick and span, make sure the lubricator is filled with oil and have one final check to ensure that everything is all right.

You will have realized that, for the larger model-engineering scales, it is the locomotive-driving that represents the great bulk of the attraction of your garden railway. Your back will ache and you will be speckled with smuts. But you wouldn't swap your railway for anything else.

# CHAPTER 15

# A Garden Railway Year

We have looked through many of the details and stratagems of garden railways. Let's bring these threads together in a more tangible form so as to get the feel of the hobby. There now follows a diary of a typical year's activities. It will be self-indulgently written from my viewpoint. People and their railways are all different, but it will serve to illustrate the sort of thing you may come to expect. I should add that I live in a corner of Wales that enjoys a mild Atlantic climate. Readers in Aberdeen or Arizona will have their own agendas.

## JANUARY

My year traditionally starts with running a train, no matter what the weather. If weather conditions are really horrible, this may consist of a battery loco hauling a couple of weighted wagons over part of the railway. But hopefully something will get steamed up, the leaves and twigs brushed away and then a long train gets a chance to stretch its legs.

Because the weeks before Christmas are usually hectic, railway maintenance may have been neglected. This is a good time to look objectively at what needs doing urgently and what can be left until warmer times. The main priority is making sure that the track is in good order. Perhaps a fishplate has slipped and the rail ends don't quite line up. Even though I don't use two-rail electrification, I still feel that urge to wipe the railtops off with fine emery cloth. Shiny rails run smoother. It also means that I have gone round my entire track and looked at every inch. Little bits of grit or twigs have

been picked out. I'm glad I have hardstanding where I walk to do this: long, wet grass can take the edge off the day.

What I am really trying to do is ensure that the railway is usable, with the minimum of outdoor work. If snow comes, I can go out and run trains straight away. There will be sunny days too, which means that I can get on with tidying up other jobs. So the emphasis is on a cosy workshop or even a tray on the knees indoors. I like to try to get on with small building and maintenance tasks early on. There have been some years where I have spent good summer months in trying to get a backlog of jobs done. Keeping the work gently ticking over, even in unpromising times, is worthwhile. But I don't see modelling jobs as a chore: they are part of the appeal. I enjoy a compulsion to make things. January is an excellent time to indulge this.

*The days can seem short and dreary at this time of the year. But we can enjoy running our trains in the same dull light that lit the full-size trains.*

## FEBRUARY

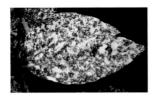

Well at least there is a hint of the days starting to lengthen. Hopefully the track is still in good working order and so trains can be run whenever the mood takes. Thoughts are turning towards building new things. Making locomotives and rolling stock is something that can go on throughout the year but making large structures and buildings needs thought. Inside the workshop they can be *big*! Things that are made of wood generate sawdust and shavings at a depressing rate. I try to do my planning and marking out indoors but then wait for a nice day to have an orgy of using power tools to cut the bits up outside. I am happy to have several jobs on the go at the same time even if it means sawing and shaping many pieces of wood for a project and then bundling them up for later.

Out of doors, I will be splashing through the puddles to check that all drainage is as it should be. It may be something as miserable as a house drain blocked with leaves or it could be something more long term – like noting an area of track that is prone to flooding in heavy rain. The garden itself is mostly dormant, so time spent in an armchair can seem appealing. There is time to think about improving, changing and tweaking; time to get inspiration from others . . . time to dream a little. But, back on earth, it is also a good time to get the paintbrushes out. Rolling stock in particular can get a worn look quite easily. There are some of us who like this but, even so, following prototype practice, we may want to touch in little scratches and chips – and re-affix odd details that have been knocked off during a busy previous year.

As mentioned earlier, I prefer to leave my buildings out all year round. But now is a good time to refresh them. Chimney pots get knocked off for a variety of reasons. Those merrily singing birds leave their calling cards on the roofs. Maybe there is some peeling paint on woodwork. However, a nice steady throughput of these background maintenance jobs means that the railway will keep the fresh sparkle of newness into the coming year. The icy winds may be blowing outside but I am snugly working away, setting the scene for another successful year. Needless to say, if I wake up to a mild sunny morning, then I am not slow to run something.

*If the track is in good running order, a sudden snow squall can be followed by running something – instead of getting cold trying to get things to work! (Photo: Phil Beckey)*

*All the usual clichés of spring hold true, I am pleased to report. (Photo: Phil Beckey)*

## MARCH

The garden is starting to come to life. In the days when I lovingly nurtured my lawn, March was the time when I would stab it viciously with a fork and sprinkle sand in the holes to help drainage. The lawnmower would give it a gentle haircut and, on a dry day, I would go round the edges with an old tenon saw to make them really sharp and neat. This really freshened everything up – making both the garden and me feel better. In deference to my advancing years, the grass has been replaced with paving slabs and raised flowerbeds but I am still a lawn man at heart. Beyond that though, this is the time for getting the garden cleaned up. There is a stirring in the air. The trains have more opportunities to run and larger projects can be looked at. Work can start on an extension of the railway or perhaps to rearrange something into a more con-

venient form. As I write these lines, foundations are going in for a longer run-round loop at a station. In the light of operational experience, changes are needed: an echo of full-size practice.

This is also the time to be thinking about travels. In early April I enjoy the annual major meeting of the 16mm Association and other dates are going in the diary. The structure of the coming months is starting to shape up. Meanwhile, the general maintenance is quietly going on in the background. In the workshop it may be something as simple as going through all the goods wagons making sure that the wheels are clean of the crud they have accumulated, and that the couplings are all intact. Outside, with the chances of frost rapidly receding, I start to think about any concrete work that needs to be done. On a long stone wall, maybe there are one or two small repairs to attend to. If a concrete building has cracked, make sure it is absolutely dry and then I may well be able to repair it with ordinary waterproof PVA glue. Masonry paint may have flaked off here or there. It is all a process of freshening up.

The weather doesn't stick rigidly to the clichés of the calendar. In late February or March there can be beautiful April days! When the rain has cleared away in late afternoon and as yellow sun streams down, a blackbird can start singing and the world seems fresh and clean. It is then that a steam engine can be at its best. In the still-damp air the steam itself is prominent and the whole train becomes a living thing. We are glad that the track is in good order and that everything runs well. One small landmark in the year is the British institution of the clocks going forward one hour. It means an extra hour of daylight to be in the garden, after a day's work. There is the time for enjoying a very personal pleasure.

## APRIL

This is like March but better! Later evenings and earlier mornings give me more opportunities to enjoy the garden. This is important to everyone who has a full working day to contend with. Being able to enjoy an hour of natural light in the evening lifts the spirit. Green things are sprouting up everywhere and it is the time when I am enthusiastic to get stuck in to major tasks outside. It is worth repeating that this is part of the hobby; not an obstacle to it. Creating a private world and maintaining it in good order is part of the appeal and, at this time of year, the juices are really flowing.

Those first meetings and get-togethers are starting to happen. Although I am not as much of a social creature as others, I still enjoy seeing the hobby from a wider perspective, meeting old friends and making new ones. Garden railways are something you never stop learning about. Some newcomers to the hobby can come up with thoughts and ideas that are really interesting. Fresh eyes can see things differently. For those of such persuasion, there are also modelling competitions to sharpen the focus. The high-precision model engineers will always inspire us but just as valuable are the simpler models. This hobby needs breadth as well as depth. If I restrict myself to my own boundaries too much, I find it easy to go stale. So at this time of year, exposure to other people's thoughts and hardware seems to give an extra zip to what I am doing in my own garden.

*The sun comes out after an April shower in this Highland scene.*

## MAY

Suddenly the trappings of summer are approaching; those long hours of daylight and the flourishing green stuff. In the past it was also a time for lawnmowing, hedge clipping and weeding. This is why I will have tried to complete most of the overall maintenance and general freshening up. Even though my garden is now low maintenance, I still like to get things looking fresh by this time of the year. Repainting things in the garden generally and washing down paths and walls: it all seems good management. Again, life is better if you do maintenance too early rather than too late. Cleaning out the pond may seem far removed from railway modelling, but both you and the fish will be happier.

I find this the month when the railway gets its most intense personal running. Ever the optimist, I reason that the rain is a bit warmer now! Everything seems so fresh and clean. There may still be major building projects in hand but trains will run. The first visitors, individuals or groups, are starting to appear. But there are still plenty of opportunities to enjoy the quieter magic of it all. In a hectic life, here is an oasis of calm. We do things more gently here – or at least I do. In early evening, at leisure, a live steam engine and a few coaches appear on the track. To get things prepared for a run takes as long as it takes. I enjoy making sure that everything is done properly at a steady pace. Checking the track for twigs and helping a snail off the track is all the better to the accompaniment of birdsong. There really is time to stand and stare.

*The first visitors appear – bringing their locomotives with them. It is good to see fresh faces.*

*Early one summer morning an engine is prepared for the day.*

## JUNE

The days have now grown long. If you are a morning person, a sunny 5.00am will show you the garden in an entirely different light – literally. Sunshine reaches places it only sees for a couple of weeks of the year. The dawn chorus will be in full swing and the rest of the world seems far away. At the other end of the clock, running a train in the very late evening afterglow has its own appeal. It is a good time to share with friends and an opportunity to visit elsewhere. It is also a good time to check that the steam-up box has all its bits and pieces correctly inside. I have learned not to take vast amounts of rolling stock and equip-

ment. A checklist of essentials is a good thing to have permanently pinned up in the workshop as I don't want to swamp someone else's layout with trains, or clutter up his garden with innumerable boxes. So an engine and a short train are as much as I will take. The camera will be with me but without any expectation of taking good railway photographs. This is more a time to record friendly occasions for the scrapbook.

But all the while, I find that the urge to build things will not be denied. Some people get the process of building a railway done and then become operators and maintainers. I am not in this group. To me, making things and running trains have an equal priority. This proportion seems to vary tremendously and you will no doubt find your own equilibrium. It will certainly affect how your practical railway year will vary from the one I am describing now.

# JULY

If you are a sociable sort of person, life will be getting hectic now. You may well be considering an open day. I find that such things are excellent for making sure that many of those outstanding jobs are done. The downside is that, if the open day is late in the year, then you can find yourself working through the summer rather than relaxing. Open days, in whatever branch of garden railways you may be involved, tend to be crammed into just a few summer Sundays. So choice may be limited if there is a risk of clashing with other events. But if possible, hold yours earlier rather than later. When everyone has gone home and the bunting has come down, the garden will be at its absolute best because of all that preparatory work. So there is time to relax and enjoy the rest of the summer, with only the grass, weeds and hedges to trim. If you have an untamed garden, you will have been busy trying to keep it under control around the railway areas. But by now, they will have got their second wind and seem to be growing out of control. Unwelcome though it may seem, keep on top of the trimming back. It is all too easy for a railway to become so overgrown in a couple of weeks that it becomes unusable. At such times it is easy to get a bit disheartened. Make a mental note to try to introduce some solid borders to problem areas by next year. That track, wandering through the rockery, would be improved by having small, concreted stone walls either side. Perhaps the biggest culprit is grass. I find that having grass close to track is a recipe for hard work by midsummer. At first I enjoy the novelty of continually trimming back with scissors – *so* like the real thing! That soon wears off. We want to enjoy these busy days as July merges into . . .

*On this warm, and very English summer Sunday, we relax with friends. (Photo: Phil Beckey)*

## AUGUST

Because of the school holidays, this seems to be a time for children. You may enjoy watching their little faces light up or you may consider that Herod was right after all. But I remember being young myself once – and the things that inspired me. So I am happy to try to put something back. Most children will just enjoy a visit and then be gone. They may have been merely fascinated by the curious notion of a railway engine that has a fire in it. But occasionally – just occasionally – there will be a child in whom something about the railway will register. You may have sowed the seed for a lifetime's interest.

Another of my favourite cameos is a late summer storm. The sky has seemed ominous all day and the air is oppressive. It goes quiet – even the birds have stopped singing. There is that same sense of expectation we get just before it starts to snow. I make a point of going round the garden to make sure I haven't left anything out during the recent dry spell. It is a good time to check the track for any flotsam. And then I wait. Sometimes it ends in an anticlimax. But if all goes well the darkness increases, the first huge raindrops crash on to the dry soil and free up that distinctive smell. The drops become continuous and then turn into a torrent. The surface of the pond is blasted, bringing freshness back to the water. The train is set in motion and I watch it from some sheltered spot, preferably at eye level. If the forces are really with me, then thunder starts to roll through those dark clouds. Amid flashes of lightning and torrential rain, the train rumbles on, oblivious. All that I have worked to build is now in full harmony with nature. To me, this is my railway at its best.

And when the storm has passed, and the pale sun comes out, water droplets sparkle everywhere. That blackbird sings with a renewed intensity and the train sits in a siding, drying off. All the work of building a garden railway has just been rewarded.

*Deep black shadows amid the heat. We may have a storm soon.*

Summer is now approaching its end. Once again I renew my determination to be ahead of maintenance next year. This month seems to dash by in the twinkling of an eye. There are visits to make and more visitors to greet; pleasurable days to be had. But already I note the nights drawing in and, at some time, I wake up one morning to a fresh chill in the air. This is something I welcome eagerly.

## SEPTEMBER

This is my favourite month of the year . . . not quite sure why. Perhaps it is the feeling of peace that returns to the garden. The social activities were enjoyable but it is nice to have my garden back again. The live steam hangs in the cooler air. Ideas and thoughts come fresh again. Nature is starting to slow down but the annual rotation of birds continues. The swifts and swallows will soon be gone and then the migrating starlings will arrive, smoking across the sky. Having a garden railway makes one sensitive to the changes in the seasons.

Having spent time in the summer getting things looking really sharp and bright means that there isn't a great deal of maintenance to be done now. Inspired by ideas from other people during the summer months, I usually plunge into new modelling projects in my haphazard way. I know many people who have immaculate workshops and who are systematic in their modelling programme. I am not like that. I remain splendidly disorganized: mostly working on the principle that, if I keep nudging away at all sorts of jobs, I am bound to make progress in the end. Whatever your particular inclination is – enjoy it. I would merely urge that, in whatever ways suit you best, you keep doing things rather than just think about them.

And time passes: very quickly. Blink and ten years have gone by since you built the first part of

*Autumnal light, when combined with steam, can give lovely cameos to treasure in the dull days of winter.*

the garden railway. In the autumn I am generally laying my plans for making life a little easier next year. Sometimes, because of over-familiarity, the railway can seem dull and uninteresting. If so, there is a useful trick: try looking at it through an angled mirror. When you see everything reversed, it has the sort of new impact that a visitor would see. Take a couple of digital photographs and flip them horizontally. Be impressed and enjoy the lift this gives.

## OCTOBER

I can't bring myself to avoid the cliché about mists and mellow fruitfulness. It is just so perfect. Here is a time for bonfires and cold mornings. Nature is slowing down and things become personal and introspective. In the distance, I hear a tractor on the stubble. Trains run more gently now. If I still brought my buildings indoors for the winter, this would be the time to do it. I collect up some of the figures and platform details. I may live in a mild area but gales blow in off the Atlantic: 16mm scale luggage trolleys usually fail their flight test.

You may have been surprised that I devoted so few words to August. But it didn't need them. A garden railway is very much an all-year activity if you want it to be. If so, you may well find – as I do – that October is much more productive than high summer. The workshop seems to be buzzing merrily, interrupted only by occasional forays outside to sweep leaves away.

*Morning sunshine is weaker now. But still the trains run.*

*Even in November there can be magical times, such as an ice-cold morning when there is not a breath of wind. Everything is very silent. We don't even have to run a train: just being there is enough.*

## NOVEMBER

And the modelling goes on. The core of the railway is still functioning well. My aim is to always be able to instantly put a battery loco on the track and set it running. I will still check the main line for leaves and twigs, but that is good housekeeping anyway. The days grow short now and I enjoy what daylight hours are available to me. The CDR timetable (which I ignore!) speaks of a winter service. The last train of the day coincides with the oncoming darkness.

It is usually around now that I bring my garden railway scrapbook up to date. There are so many memories tied up in little pieces of paper. It somehow seems wrong to be too complicated with such things. I just stick accumulated odds and ends into a book – maybe with a vague chronological order, maybe not. Here is the real flavour of what makes my railway unique, as yours will be to you. My story is written in old stock lists, receipts, whimsical paperware, labels, doodles and exhibitor passes. These are the sweepings of a life with garden railways, collected up and glued in one place. It is nicely satisfying.

# DECEMBER

This is a tricky month to negotiate. There are often severe outbreaks of shopping and other pre-Yuletide horrors, so enjoy any opportunities to run trains in the garden that come your way. Jobs in the workshop can be at different levels. Nipping out for short periods and doing a bit of modelling is an excellent stress buster. This is also the time to prepare for the onslaught to come. It is worth dropping hints that certain railway items would be a welcome surprise on Christmas Day, but it would be a mistake to hold your hopes too high.

Christmas Day is particularly difficult. You are expected to come in from the workshop allegedly to 'enjoy yourself'. You may even have to take your overalls off! This is not nature's way but sometimes there is no avoiding it. One possible line of defence is to have a shoebox and a tray secreted in the house somewhere so that a spot of illicit modelling is possible. Try to impress upon the family that running a train on Christmas Day and Boxing Day is an old tradition. You may not get away with it but it's worth a try.

And then, suddenly, the year is approaching its end. The seasons have come and gone whether the railway is full-size or if it is small, like the one in my garden. We have created something in time and space.

*A seasonal Christmas card is obligatory.*

## CHAPTER 16

# Gallery

*(Photo: Marc Horovitz)*

## AMERICAN DRAMA

On his North Table Creek garden railroad, Marty Cozad has captured a real sense of the original. A long track winds through the landscape and here, in this photograph, there is a splendid arid feel to everything. Height is exploited in a different way, using the dramatic bridge to soar way above the hillside. The train is shrunk by its surroundings. It is 1:29th scale, standard gauge and is battery-powered, with radio control operation.

The sloping scree is an excellent device for dis-

playing appropriate plants. In the lush conditions of the UK, far from Nebraska, it would make sense to put an impermeable membrane down, and then put the final layer of rock and soil over that. Errant wild grasses would ruin this sort of garden. A mulch of chopped bark would also make for low maintenance, whilst still looking right for the location. If I were tackling this, I would need to ask advice on the sorts of small shrubs and plants that would be suitable for stony conditions.

One nice option for a hillside like this is to put an irregular but wide concrete channel down part of the area before covering with rocks and gravel. Circulating water can then appear to trickle randomly in small streams down the slopes.

The viaduct is a superb piece of modelling but, for a newcomer, there are simpler alternatives. A timber trestle bridge, made from stripwood, would span the ravine nicely. I might be inclined to make the handrails at the top slightly over scale, to catch a derailed train as the bottom of the gorge looks an awfully long way down. There is also a possible hazard from windy conditions that can blow rolling stock off the track at exposed locations.

With a scene as rugged as this, it is the natural landscape that is the focus of attention. Here is wilderness. That being the case, my feeling is that it wants to be left like this. Everything is just right with this scene. Adding further details or buildings simply to fill up the space would detract from it all. As the sun moves across the sky the shadow of the bridge creeps realistically across the open spaces. The whole scene is a pleasure in its own right. And into this comes a train. There is a sense of harmony and balance. It is all as it should be.

*(Photo: Paul Cooper)*

## MAINLINE MAGIC

The 2½in gauge is a fascinating mixture of possibilities. Early days were a mixture of crude steam toys and fully engineered passenger-hauling machines. The ability to haul real people is still exploited by a small number of folk today. Speaking as someone who has struggled with the weight of larger scale live steam, I champion this gauge at every possible opportunity! At the other extreme, small battery-powered locos can haul a few wagons in a small space – and remain innocent of any engineering requirements.

But in-between comes the ambience of gauge 3. Curves tend to be that bit more sweeping and the track layouts do not have to be complex. Because live steam is frequently used, tracks are often at high level for convenient access. And so to this picture.

Here we can see the magnificence of an express train, gleaming in the sunlight. There is a bulk and magnificence to it all, isn't there? But you have to be there to see this in motion – alive and breathing. The safety valve is blowing off as the whole train thunders down the track. You have to be there to get the real smell of the smoke. You have to be there to hear the urgent, but tiny, drumming of the train wheels. And if you are there, you could well become instantly addicted.

This isn't the easiest form of garden railways to get into. There are no convenient train sets that will give this perfection instantly. But given membership of the Gauge 3 Group for advice, anything is possible. There is something majestic about this scale that is hard to define. Look at the picture again and get the feeling of this train rushing all down a long summer afternoon.

## THE ULTIMATE DRIVING EXPERIENCE

Model engineers do things differently. It is the engine itself that is the alpha and omega. Everything else is usually just functional support to make the driving experience complete. In the main, the locomotive isn't really a model at all: it is a complete steam engine in its own right. There are one or two compromises that have to be made because nature can't always be scaled down. But these are not too apparent externally and, anyway, it doesn't really matter. Just look at the smile on the face of the driver. By the end of the day, there will be some smuts on that jacket but the smile will be even broader.

Note how the passenger trolley sits astride the track with footrests for stability and comfort. It is all very functional, but note too just how imposing the engine looks. It will demand good driving and firing technique: no switch-on-and-go here. But the end result is the total interaction between driver and loco, which is at the very heart of this form of garden railways.

## SMALL IS GOOD TOO

For a true garden railway in a really confined space, 0.16.5 is worth thinking about. What you see in the picture could be fitted into a space of roughly 6 × 4ft (2 × 1.5m). A circle of track can go round a pond and a waterfall in that area. Built up on a brick plinth, the layout is free from invasive weeds and grass, hence maintenance is low. The fish sport amongst the water lilies and the bees hum over the tiny flowers. It all sits nicely on the eye.

The track is Peco 0.16.5, but when it is bedded in the landscape, it is difficult to tell from ordinary 00 or H0 track, which has the same gauge. Incidentally, you will note a bit of 0-gauge standard gauge track in the foreground, and how it makes the narrow gauge look narrow. The locos are battery-powered but ordinary two-rail works just fine. This also has the benefit that ordinary 00-gauge trains can be run at any time, provided one ignores the out-of-scale buildings.

The coach bodies were built in plastic card by Dave Pinniger and they run on ordinary Hornby wagon chassis. One of the principal attractions of this scale is that cheap and reliable 4mm scale equipment can be incorporated into the narrow gauge models.

So let us just lose ourselves in the picture for a moment. On a baking hot summer afternoon, a narrow gauge train shuffles past the old standard gauge railway station. The shade of that canopy would be welcome right now. Even better would be to sit near to the small waterfall we can hear not far away. Daydreams can come in small packages too.

*(Photo courtesy:* Die Gartenbahn*)*

## CONTINENTAL SIMPLICITY

Not everyone wants a garden railway that is hand crafted or which represents ultimate realism. The sheer pleasure of simply running trains is as strong as it ever was. And there are garden railways that can cater for this. In this illustration virtually every-thing is bought over the counter and simply assem-bled according to clear instructions. This mainly LGB Continental layout will run reliably in all weathers. It can run to a timetable and host visiting matching trains. So it has a lot going for it.

The track segments mostly just clip together and the wiring is particularly simple. The trains will run straight out of the box. However, they may well come with instructions. Please, I beg you – do read these. With a layout like this, it is common practice to keep the rolling stock unweathered and stored carefully in the original boxes. The model trains are considered objects of virtue in their own right. In the G-Scale Society you will find many a kindred spirit with this viewpoint.

But above all, here is a railway system that any-one can put together and enjoy. The static photo-graph cannot convey the pleasure of seeing a train gliding across the garden. There have been many garden railways around the world that started with a circle of LGB track around the Christmas tree. Be prepared to succumb to such tempta-tions.

*(Photo: Geoff Culver)*

## ELEGANT SINUOSITY

Summertime in a large garden, and the living seems rather easy right now. The layout is functional because it is the complete train that holds our attention. We have come together to enjoy our mutual delight in such things. Here is gauge 1 at its most elegant. It sounds so silky, gliding past. Those reverse curves somehow add to the feel of the real thing and also make the complete track foundations more stable. Our eyes can, at will, blot out everything that is not the moving train. It is afternoons such as this that are long remembered. In different guises they have been enjoyed since Victorian times. This photograph shows us why. There is no bustle. It is a very English afternoon.

## 'WELL MET BY MOONLIGHT'

A steam train by moonlight can be quite a dull subject. It is mostly shadows and suggestion. This seems to work best as a solitary pleasure. Visitors falling over things in the darkness detract from the peace of the event somehow. On a really still night, sounds are magnified. Somewhere in the distance a dog is barking – you hear it so clearly. Your train too is sounding right. The exhaust beats are sharp and the metal wheels are drumming along the track, perhaps with the chain couplings tinkling slightly. This sound changes as the track goes over bridges, through tunnels and behind bushes. These sounds are always there unconsciously, but at night they have an extra significance. You can pick out exactly where the train is from those subtle changes.

The day may have been hot and sultry but now the coolness in the air is particularly welcome. Armed with just a torch (or even better, a real oil lamp); you will guide this train to a stop at the end of its run: the last train of the day. The engine will be uncoupled and run to the shed for disposal. When all is done, the door is closed and you remember to turn out the lights. Yes: truly a solitary pleasure.

*(Photo: Alan Walker)*

## YES, THAT'S HOW IT REALLY WAS

Alan Walker created this exquisite cameo – with the help of time. If the picture looks like an old railway that has seen many winters and summers, that's because it is. Or rather, it was. We see the last days of a railway built many years ago. Knowing that it was due for rebuilding one day, the maintenance lapsed somewhat. Here is the world of the Corris railway in its last days. The weathering was done by nature. Everything has the real patina of age and neglect.

I can just remember the Talyllyn railway in pre-preservation days. This photograph captures the essence of that perfectly. The railways of today are, in the main, beautifully kept by people that have a love of them and pride in their work. This is as it should be. But of the old lines, we have only some black-and-white photographs, a few memories and maybe an occasional picture of a model, just like this. Here the garden railway says something to us about times long gone. It may be skilled modelling or perhaps just happenstance. We can lose ourselves in the hazy sunny morning when nothing is stirring. For some, it is more than enough.

## ATMOSPHERE PERSONIFIED

The dust jacket of this book shows a stretch of track on a cool morning. We have just seen that same area in all seasons and even in moonlight. We create our landscapes and run our trains – and every day – sometimes every hour – we see things differently. It is fitting then that we shall conclude with a picture of one of those perfect moments. It is Midsummer's Eve and a special train is being run. The sun, although low in the sky in the late evening, is still hot. The dust in the air glows red and gold and, already, the harvest is well under way.

The train bursts out of the tunnel and under a footbridge over a deep cutting. It is a living thing, breathing and swaying through the evening. We imagine that there could be a keg of beer on board the first coach – ensuring that the singing will be enthusiastic if not always melodic. We have talked about many practical things, but perhaps this is a good point to take our leave: just enjoying the magic of the atmosphere.

## AND FINALLY . . .

Our exploration of the nuts and bolts of garden railways is now complete. We have looked at the practicalities and we have considered options and alternatives. The conclusion is that we all have our own tastes and priorities and that there are different ways of achieving them. I hope too that it has become clear that there is nothing here that is particularly daunting. You can build or buy to whatever degree of complexity you feel comfortable with. The people that have built garden railways in the past did so because they wanted it enough. Today, there is good trade support and there is a body of experience that has been built up. It is an ongoing process. You, in turn, will add to that as your own railway comes into being. I wish you well with it – and that it gives you the same immense reward and satisfaction that it has to so many others. The journey continues . . .

# Principal Manufacturers and Suppliers

Producing a list of suppliers is something of a minefield. Companies come and go, change addresses or even ownership. This applies particularly to smaller firms and individuals who make items for sale in their garden shed. What follows is a general guide only to point you in suitable directions. You will notice that I frequently suggest joining the appropriate society for your intended scale and reading the model railway press. You will find both to be sources of a wealth of information.

All the equipment is available from specialist trading stores in the UK, USA and Europe. I will restrict myself to giving website addresses only. Check the model railway press for postal addresses and phone numbers.

## CONTINENTAL G SCALE

LGB – www.lgb.de – is the leading supplier of everything you need to build a durable, fuss-free garden railway. Expensive in the UK, the outline will be either continental European or American. Everything is made chunky and reliable. If you are moving up to this scale from working in 00 gauge indoors, things may seem crude and shiny. But in the larger vista of the garden this is much diminished, and you may consider that the heavy build quality is worth having. For realism, try to avoid the sharper radius curves.

Pola – www.faller.de – and Piko – www.piko.de – produce building kits and accessories that are in tune with what LGB has to offer. Everything is simple and rugged and forms a particularly good resource for the beginner, as well as a basis for more serious conversions, including anglicizing the appearance of some models. Can seem expensive in the UK for simple plastic kits but you get strong components that resist the effects of ultraviolet light and extreme weather conditions.

Preiser is where the matching figures come from. Prices are high in the UK compared, for example, to 16mm scale.

Marklin – www.marklin.com – provide 1:32nd scale standard gauge equipment.

A browse through a recent copy of *Railway Modeller*, *Continental Modeller* or *Garden Rail*; *Garden Railways* (USA) and *Die Gartenbahn* (Germany) will give you useful starting points for addresses.

In addition, there are many small European manufacturers of G-scale equipment. For example, try investigating Ranger, Hochwertige Zinnfiguren, Brawa, Prehm-modellbahn, and Dingler on the Internet or look for their advertisements in *Die Gartenbahn* magazine. The G-Scale Society is also an excellent point of contact.

## AMERICAN G SCALE

Bachmann – www.bachmanntrains.com – (*see* also 0 gauge) is the principal supplier of American G-scale items, all of which are listed on their website. Manufactured in the Far East, prices tend to be low. This equipment forms the basis of many a garden railway. Bachmann also produce a nice range of 0n30 (a sort of 0.16.5) equipment that is very suitable for a compact garden railway.

Hartland Locomotive Works www.H-L-W.com – produces a compatible range of American G-scale equipment.

Accucraft – www.accucraft.com – (*see* also British 16mm scale) offers further similar alternatives plus the option of a range of live steam locomotion. They also make 1:32nd scale standard gauge products, running on G-scale track.

Several US manufacturers make standard gauge products to 1:29th scale, running on G-scale track (and may use a term like G-gauge to describe it). The much larger size of the prototypes, combined with the smaller scale, often produces a model that is similar in bulk to proper G-scale narrow gauge. It is only when you see the size of a model engine driver that the difference is brought home!

Aristo-Craft – www.aristocraft.com – and USA Trains – www.usatrains.com – make a splendid broad range of standard gauge equipment to this 1:29th scale. USA Trains also make narrow gauge prototypes to 1:24th scale. However, the different scales are clearly flagged up in their literature and on the website.

Railking 1 Gauge Trains – www.railking1gauge.com – offer 1:32nd scale locos and rolling stock.

There is a huge support market of smaller manufacturers in the USA and I recommend reading a copy of *Garden Railways* magazine for access to these, together with substantial lists of general traders. *Steam in the Garden* magazine concentrates on the more technical live steam aspects.

## BRITISH 16MM SCALE

Roundhouse – www.roundhouse-eng.com – supply a good range of practical live steam locomotives that start with simple functional examples and go up to larger fine-scale models. Highly regarded in the hobby.

Accucraft – www.accucraft.com – (*see* also American G scale) make a range of live steam locomotives and wagons in tune with British 16mm scale in the garden.

Mamod is a name you may encounter. Large numbers of their simple tank engines have been produced in the past. In theory, these should have been a good, cheap entry into the hobby but there has been a very chequered history of company ownership and, at times, such poor quality control that some engines could not work as bought.

PPS Steam Models – www.pps-steam-models.co.uk – oscillating cylinder technology has found a good home here.

There are a number of smaller companies that build live steam locos and details will be found in the model railway press. In fact, this branch of the hobby supports a huge array of small businesses and individuals that make all sorts of things. Joining the 16mm Association opens up a whole world of new products.

Tenmille – www.tenmille.co.uk – produces a range of track, kits and accessories in 16mm/G scale and also, as the name suggests, in 10mm scale: gauge 1.

Peco – www.peco-uk.com – (*see* also 0 gauge and gauge 1) supply a comprehensive range of tracks in many scales and gauges.

Many 16mm products, from companies large and small, are available through specialist dealers some of whom also make their own products.

Brandbright – www.brandbright.co.uk – have had a long-term close association with the hobby.

Garden Railway Specialists – www.grsuk.com – (*see* also gauge 3) supply in-house products for British outline G scale as well as being a more general dealer.

## 0 GAUGE

Home of 0 gauge – www.ogauge.co.uk – a useful source of materials and kits.

Bachmann – www.bachmanntrains.com – (*see* also American G scale) produces a small range of ready-to-run brass locomotives and stock.

Lima produced some cheap, plastic-based, equipment in the past.

Peco – www.peco-uk.com – (*see* also British 16mm scale and gauge 1) will provide the track system. There is also a limited amount of continental equipment to be had.

In the UK, this hobby tends to be the preserve of the kitbuilder and the model maker. The greater part is focused on electric pick-up from the track with close attention to fine detail. To get an insight into all of this, I suggest joining the Gauge 0 Guild.

The modern replicas of Bassett-Lowke equipment have a charm about them and this is taken further with Messrs ACE trains that have a truly nostalgic tinplate look. ETS trains are also in this genre and a browse through the model press will provide details.

## GAUGE 1

Aster – www.asterhobbies.co.uk – is the major player in this scale. They produce live steam locomotives and kits in 1:32 scale. At any one time the range is limited, but is constantly being changed. At first glance to modellers used to 00 gauge indoors, prices of some can seem eye-watering, but they are exquisite scale models and represent good value for money.

Peco – www.peco-uk.com – (*see* also British 16mm scale and 0 gauge) and Tenmille www.tenmille. co.uk – (*see* also British 16mm scale), also supply gauge 1 equipment.

Wagon and Carriage Works – www.wagonand carriage.co.uk – is an excellent source of what is available.

There is a support trade of small manufacturers, including etched-brass kits. You would do well to join the Gauge 1 Society to investigate them.

## GAUGE 3

Garden Railway Specialists – www.grsuk.com – (*see* also British 16mm scale) supply in-house products as well as being a more general dealer.

For a simple introduction to this scale (also known as 2½in gauge or G64), look for items and kits that are suitable for the modeller rather than the model engineer. This is yet another scale where I would recommend that you should join the appropriate group. In earlier pages I have said that this represents the 'standard gauge' against which the narrow gauge of G scale can be set. Gauge 3 is somewhat underscale (and under-gauge) to be the correct big brother of 16mm scale, but some people can live with this anomaly.

There is also a more model-engineering aspect to this gauge, using 17/32in scale. It is characterized by traditional methods of building locomotives from castings and raw materials. Because larger engineering scales have become more popular, there seems to be a reservoir of unfinished projects and sets of parts. Unless you have some experience in model engineering, avoid being tempted by bargains in this area.

# Groups and Associations

In Europe and the USA, there is a tendency for groups to be based around a particular product or magazine, LGB being a good example. There are many groups devoted to particular prototypes in different countries, some of which have modelling subsections. But in the UK, there are some strong associations devoted to a particular scale, often appropriate to the garden railway. There are also plenty of spin-off e-groups relating to specific areas. I will restrict myself to giving website addresses only. Check the model press for postal addresses and phone numbers.

The Gauge 0 Guild – www.gauge0guild.com – is a very popular group. There is a predominant leaning towards indoor modelling, much of it of very high quality, but there is much here of value to the garden railway enthusiast in this scale. The house magazine is very useful and the website has many valuable links.

The G-Scale Society – www.g-scale-society.co.uk – caters for both indoor and outdoor layouts and it is a good way into a world of 'easy' garden railways, where much of the technicalities have been ironed out, enabling a complete novice to start his journey

to a successful railway out of doors. The society also has an active exhibition and social calendar, details of which may be found on the website.

The 16mm Association – www.16mm. org.uk – is a large, well-run organization that seems to aim specifically at garden railways, without actually meaning to. There is an excellent bi-monthly house magazine and also a newsletter. This group represents a large resource of friendly help and advice, together with an active social scene.

The Gauge 1 Model Railway Association (GIMRA) – www.gaugeone.org – is the guardian of this historic scale. There is coverage of traditional engineering projects as well as a good reflection of what modern trade support is available.

The Gauge 3 Society – www.gauge3.co.uk – caters for this magnificent scale. Although small in number (and possibly because of this), it is a splendidly friendly and helpful group bonded by a love of the heroically sized models that they run.

For model engineered, passenger-hauling railways the technology is universal. So the clubs, which act as a focus for useful bodies of experience, are usually regional and based on club tracks.

# Further Study

A mainstream model railway magazine, such as *Railway Modeller*, will provide contact addresses for the various groups associated with particular scales of model railway. In particular, the G-Scale Society and the 16mm Association provide huge amounts of information, both in their glossy magazines and with online resources. In the UK there is a magazine devoted to garden railways called *Garden Rail*. In Germany there is the excellent *Die Gartenbahn*, which reflects the developing European approach to garden railways. But by far and away the biggest magazine is the US *Garden Railways*. It concentrates on US garden railway practice but is a tremendous source of reference (with a great deal of valuable information about miniature plants in particular) whatever your inclination may be. The USA is also the home of *Steam in the Garden* magazine. As its title suggests, it tends to concentrate on the technicalities of small-scale live steam.

There are also magazines for model engineers. In the UK, these are *Model Engineer* and *Engineering in Miniature*, whereas the title of note in the USA is *Live Steam*. With these, the emphasis is really on the technical engineering side, rather than on garden railways.

Books about garden railways have been limited. Some of these are quite old and dated, and some may be out of print. But here is a list of titles to look out for:

Boreham, D., *Narrow Gauge Railway* (MAP) c1970
Evans, M., *Outdoor Model Railways* (MAP) 1970
Freezer, C. J., *The Garden Railway Manual* (PSL) 1995
Gorton, T. (ed.), *Garden Railways in Focus* (Atlantic) 2005
Gorton, T., *Steam in the Garden* (Atlantic) 2005
Jackson-Stevens, E., *Scale Model Electric Tramways* (David & Charles) c1972
Jones, P., *Garden Railway Guides Booklets* (Brandbright) c1990
Jones, P., *Model Railway Constructor Special, Number 8* (Ian Allan) 1987
Neale, D., *Railways in the Garden* (Peco) 1978
Ray, J., *A Lifetime with 0 Gauge* (Atlantic) 1992

Kalmbach (www.trains.com) are a useful source of publications.

There are also some useful 'shows-you-how' videos and DVDs available. But the best way to study the subject further is to talk to people. Have a look at various types of garden railways to gain a broad picture of the subject.

# Garden Railway Photography

All the normal rules of good photography apply but there are several other things that you need to think about when trying to record the railway. The most important is to overcome the fact that your eyes have an ability to concentrate on the main things and ignore the rest. You don't see the dustbins behind the station or the knees next to a train. The camera does. Unless there is something momentous happening, never be tempted to randomly snap things. Take time, on your own, to think about every shot, and try to get right down to train level wherever possible. Quality photography does not demand expensive cameras: just a thoughtful photographer.

This applies even more to making videos. In all the excitement, good practice can go out the window and the result will be unsatisfactory. A couple of good minutes are so much better than an hour of painful viewing. Common practice is to adapt a flat wagon to carry a camera and this gives you a record of the driver's view. Set the camera on a wide angle, but even with this, there is a tendency for corners to suddenly loom up in the finished shot. Mounting the camera on a small turntable on the wagon can provide a more professional effect. An arm reaches out forward of this to a weighted bogie, some inches ahead of the vehicle (but not quite in shot). Thus the camera always turns slightly into curves before reaching them. The result is a much smoother transition.

However, there is a practical simple option on offer. A modest digital camera or a mobile phone that can take images often has a simple video option. The resolution won't be wonderful but it costs little to strap either of these on to a wagon with an elastic band for a simple view from the cab. Moreover, the file is so small that it is easily sent to friends via the Internet.

# Lollipops

Over and above all of the mechanics of building a garden railway, you may want to allow yourself one or two extras. They may be flights of fancy, bits of theatre or even follies. A sign saying 'To the Trains' is something that may raise a smile. You may have one or two railway relics that could perhaps be built into those raised walls. If a moderately raised track crosses a path, then why not let your imagination flow, and build a proper brick or stone overbridge? And whilst you are at it, put up some suitable warning signs.

There may be opportunities for one or two special effects. Perhaps I could quote a couple of my own examples. In a model of a Victorian waterworks, as well as the existing mechanical gubbins to circulate water, I have a modern pump house. This is lit inside and also contains a substantial electric motor, mounted on a sounding-board and driving a fan. Its sole purpose is to produce a scaled-down sound of the real thing. On a more ambitious scale, my steelworks features a coking plant. Inside this is a bulkhead housing containing a fireglow bulb, together with a small disco fog machine. At night, the sky over that part of the garden is lit up with great fiery clouds of steam. It is both splendidly theatrical and silly at the same time.

I happen to enjoy inventing such things but understand that other people may not share my eccentricity. However, if you want to try something unusual, then go ahead and do it. Being conventional all the time is a dull option. Remember: it is your imagination that will contribute to the broadening of this hobby.

# Index